Critical Theory and Classroom Talk

Multilingual Matters

Bicultural and Trilingual Education
  MICHAEL BYRAM and JOHAN LEMAN (eds)
Breaking the Boundaries
  EUAN REID and HANS H. REICH (eds)
Child Language Disability
  KAY MOGFORD and JANE SADLER (eds)
Deaf-ability — Not Disability
  WENDY McCRACKEN and HILARY SUTHERLAND
Dialect and Education
  J. CHESHIRE, V. EDWARDS, H. MUNSTERMANN & B. WELTENS (eds)
Emerging Partnerships: Current Research in Language and Literacy
  DAVID WRAY (ed.)
ESL: A Handbook for Teachers and Administrators in International Schools
  EDNA MURPHY
Gender in Education
  EILEEN M. BYRNE (ed.)
Key Issues in Bilingualism and Bilingual Education
  COLIN BAKER
Language Policy Across the Curriculum
  DAVID CORSON
The Management of Change
  PAMELA LOMAX (ed.)
Managing Staff Development in Schools
  PAMELA LOMAX (ed.)
Minority Education: From Shame to Struggle
  T. SKUTNABB-KANGAS and J. CUMMINS (eds)
One Europe — 100 Nations
  ROY N. PEDERSEN
Oral Language Across the Curriculum
  DAVID CORSON
The Path to Language: Bilingual Education for Deaf Children
  DANIELLE BOUVET
Parents on Dyslexia
  S. VAN DER STOEL (ed.)
Performance Indicators
  C. T. FITZ-GIBBON (ed.)
Story as Vehicle
  EDIE GARVIE

Please contact us for the latest book information:
Multilingual Matters,
Bank House, 8a Hill Road,
Clevedon, Avon BS21 7HH,
England

THE LANGUAGE AND EDUCATION LIBRARY 2
Series Editor: David Corson

Critical Theory and Classroom Talk

Robert Young

MULTILINGUAL MATTERS LTD
Clevedon • Philadelphia • Adelaide

To my Father
Bruce Corrie Young

Library of Congress Cataloging in Publication Data

Young, Robert, 1940–
Critical Theory and Classroom Talk/Robert Young
(The Language and Education Library: 2)
Includes bibliographical references and index.
1. Interaction analysis in education. 2. Critical theory. 3. Habermas,
Jurgen. 4. Education — Philosophy. I. Title. II. Series.
LB1034.Y58   1991
371.1'022   dc20

British Library Cataloguing in Publication Data

A CIP catalogue record for this book is available from the British Library

ISBN 1-85359-126-2
ISBN 1-85359-125-4 (pbk)

Multilingual Matters Ltd

UK: Bank House, 8a Hill Road, Clevedon, Avon BS21 7HH, England.
USA: 1900 Frost Road, Suite 101, Bristol, PA 19007, USA.
Australia: P.O. Box 6025, 83 Gilles Street, Adelaide, SA 5000, Australia.

Index compiled by Meg Davies (Society of Indexers)
Typeset by Editorial Enterprises, Torquay.
Printed and bound in Great Britain by the Longdunn Press Ltd.

Contents

Glossary of Terms

Criticism	Often used here in the colloquial sense of saying something negative about something.
Critical Theory	The theory of critique
Critique	Appraisal, identification of *both* good and bad points of something.
Epistemology	The study of the nature of knowledge; more specifically, of the conditions under which a knower is justified in holding a proposition to be warranted. This is contrasted by Habermas with the science of knowledge, or Critical Theory, which studies the whole process and nature as knower of the-species-which-knows, *homo sapiens*.
Ideology Critique	Critique first of all of structures of meaning-making that serve the existential interests of some part of the social group rather than all its members; also critique of the meanings made.
Illocution	Roughly, what is said when someone says something; the 'content'.
Interests	The needs and wants of socially defined groups or categories of people. Some of these may be based in absolute needs, such as the need for a minimum amount of food; others may be socially desirable or fashionable house, car etc.
Ontology	The study of what exists; derivatively, someone's beliefs about what exists.
Perlocution	Roughly, what someone seeks to achieve *by* saying some particular content; the thing achieved *through* (per) saying something, e.g. to make someone angry by saying something insulting.

Pheonmenology

The study of how the world is perceived, irrespective of whether what is perceived actually exists or not, or whether it exists in quite the same way as it is perceived to.

Pragmatics

The study of language as a medium of doing or accomplishing things, from conveying a meaning to condemning someone to death; the study of language use.

Problem

Following Dewey, a problem is defined as a *situation* in which human adaptation has failed. This can be as simple as turning on the kitchen tap to find no water coming out or as complex as finding that the by-products of affluent societies are killing us and the planet.

Problematic

Roughly, the set of problems as perceived by an individual or group. The situation insofar as things are not working out.

Proposition

This is a difficult notion. It is an aspect of meaning, roughly, the state of affairs presumed, implied or stated to be the case. It is usually a mistake to try to treat propositional meaning independently from other layers of meaning of the utterances which indicate them.

Relevance

Being related to the wants and needs of individuals or groups, or perceived to be.

Token

When we make word noises we never make them exactly the same way twice. How is it that we can recognise that on different occasions we are saying the same word? We take the approximate noise (or scribble) as a token of a type. Usually, it is the token of more than one type. An utterance may give an indication of (be a token for) a set of words which form a grammatical sentence in a language (a sentence-type) and at the same time, through the way it is spoken, or other aspects of its relation to context, give other tokens. For instance, the placing of emphasis on a particular word may give a token that it belongs to the type 'important word' or 'new information'.

Type

A set of objects, relationships or processes grouped together by some rule and constituted by the set of its tokens. A type is judged by its usefulness for some analytical purpose.

Universalisation

The process through which an idea, a problem solution, a belief or a moral principle becomes the possession of all members of the species. The significance of this is related to Kant's idea that we could accept moral principles only if we were able to say that they could be a general law for everyone and that we would be happy for everyone to behave the same way as we do in the matter under discussion. For Kant, this was a corollary of the principle of treating all human beings with respect and not as mere means to other people's ends.

Utterance

An event in which we make meaning and convey it by speaking, writing or otherwise producing a string of signs at a particular time and in a particular place.

1 World–Education–Future

What this book is about

This book is about the way relationships between teachers and learners are expressed through language. It is about the form such relationships must take if they are to enhance the power of learners to solve problems. And it is about the kind of relationships which are best suited to promoting improvement in the problem-solving power of the global community.

In it you will encounter a thing usually called 'Critical Theory'. The use of this term creates difficulties because it is now widely misunderstood. It would be much easier simply to call the process by a name that more closely expresses the truth of the thing — Theory and Practice of Critique — but that would mean that a term in use for more than 70 years would have to be abandoned. I will also talk about 'education', but that word will not simply mean schooling or 'something-to-do-with-teaching'. It will mean any deliberate process which enhances the problem-solving power of learners. I need still more words to complete the basic list I will have to use. I need some word to name the attempt to make sure that the problem-solving power of learners has a real chance of eventually becoming greater than that of the teachers: I will call this kind of progress or development 'evolution'. I will have to talk about the gradual process of 'globalisation' of problem solving which is occurring as more and more nations and their leaders recognise that the limitations of our planetary environment's capacity to absorb the results of competitive economic growth between nations are near at hand: I will call this the 'universalisation' of problem solving.

I also need to talk about 'rationality'. There are many definitions of this notion. My definition is only a pointer rather than a detailed map, but I think of rationality as 'clear thinking' or 'thinking which improves our understanding of things *and* our actions'. This idea of rationality is broader than some philosophers' technical definitions, which want to tie it to the theories of natural science or to symbolic logic and separate it radically from the notion of practice. I believe it makes sense to call something 'rational' if it has the characteristics of clear thinking and better thinking and action in accordance with this. For instance, I would call someone rational who said they didn't like the government and then voted against it at the next election. I would call someone rational who said they believed in honesty and then I saw them draw a shopkeeper's attention to the fact that they had been given a dollar too much in their change. And I would call someone rational who thought about something, came to a conclusion contrary to his or her previous beliefs and then at least began to question those previous beliefs. So I would wish to capture for 'rationality' some of the meaning usually associated with the word 'reasonableness', but I would want to go beyond mere thinking to action based on it.

If we think of critical theory as theory of critique, it has several advantages. It makes it a little easier to remember that critical theory is more appropriately thought of as critical *method*. It also lets us see the links between critique in the area of natural and social science and critique in areas such as morality, art and literature. It also provides a defence against the attempt by mainstream Western Marxists to hijack the term to describe their particular line of criticism of capitalism. And it lets us remember that critique can be positive as well as negative — literary critique, for instance, is a form of appraisal, of identifying strengths as well as weaknesses. Talk of problem-solving power rather than acquiring knowledge is another important distinction. This has two advantages: it lets us plug into Dewey's educational thinking, which is still very useful and powerful, and it makes it quite clear that the only gap between education and life is the accidental and temporary one which intervenes between all preparation to do something and the actual doing.

Dewey's thinking is valuable because it promotes just the kind of redefinition of problems that we need today. By treating problems as systemic things — as a configuration of pieces that don't fit together, or as a *situation* — Dewey lets us see solutions in the same terms. Many of our present problems have been created by an externalising approach to problems. In trying to solve problems, we have traditionally looked towards an external manipulation of our environment through new technology — the technological fix — rather than to, say, an inward change of our attitudes. This is human enough. The 'problem' is always the other person, not ourselves, the tools, not the craftsperson. In evolving beyond the medieval world view, we both gained and lost. We lost the sense of inwardness, and gained control and power of an external kind. Perhaps it is time to recover a sense of the whole.

Universalisation and evolution go together. It's because we are becoming one world and because this confronts us with new kinds of problems which old problem-solving methods can't handle that we need to have education which aims to equip each new generation of learners with problem-solving powers beyond those of the old generation which is teaching them.

All human societies have had to cope with what Hanna Arendt, in *The Human Condition*[1] called 'natality' — the business of inculcating newcomers into the way of the tribe. In environmentally and technologically static societies, this could consist of a set of educative practices which passed on the problem-solving methods of the older generation (along with their associated attitudes, beliefs, skills etc.). But if the relationship of the society to its environment is changing, through changing technology, changing organisation of the process of using environmental resources, or changes in the environment itself, the old problem-solving methods may not be enough. In the past, societies which faced change had to adapt their problem-solving methods on the wing, or suffer uncontrolled change, often severe. For instance, one common change in the environment of a society might be the arrival on its borders of a group of war-like strangers. When Attila brought his armies to the gates of Rome he brought uncontrolled and drastic change. But however severe the changes brought about in the past by such things as conquest, drought, the mechanisation of agriculture or the rise of systematic commerce, they were relatively benign when we compare them with the scale and potential destructiveness of the changes our children are likely to have to face in the twenty-first century.

Human societies also have to deal with the problem of multiple perspectives. They must create some common ground among individuals and bridge the gap which is created by the fact that each of us sees things slightly differently most of the time, and considerably differently when our existential interests diverge from those of others (existential interests roughly = situated wants and needs). In our present global problem of resource limitation and world pollution we must, for the first time, establish this common ground between different cultures. This is universalisation. It is also simply a necessary ingredient of effective problem solving, since a solution isn't a solution unless it is universalised. Less than that and you run the risk of one-sided, colonialist solutions, which reflect the interests of one group and merely displace the problem rather than solve it.

Hanna Arendt's third great insight was that the human condition is basically symbolic — we are meaning makers. We live in terms of our stories about the world. Making sense of our experiences and actions is as necessary to us as food and shelter. Our stories, narratives, theories — call them what you will — are one of the things that separates us from the animals. Because we have them, we can tell them to others, bridging the gulf between minds, we can tell them to the children, bridging the gap between generations, and we can change them, reconstruct them or abandon them, and so change the courses of action associated with them, thus coping with new situations and new experiences.

In our present situation it is clear that knowledge useful in the past, problem-solving methods that once worked, will not be enough. Some of what the
older generation has to offer may still be useful, some methods of problem
solving may still work, but other old knowledge, other old attitudes, other old
skills may have to be abandoned. And new attitudes, knowledge, and skills
will have to be developed — by the new generation. The school curriculum
will have to give reality to words that have been used for many years with little real attention — creativity, adaptability, innovation. Teaching will have to
become evolutionary. Evolutionary problem solving is, in a way, saying too
much. Genuine problem solving is inherently evolutionary, since problems can
never be solved once and for all. We can make changes in the configuration
of things, including changes in our own attitudes, but other changes will also
occur, renewing the imperative to adapt, to solve new problems. Education for
life, if that phrase means anything, is education for reflective change and
adaptation of the self, for co-operative change in relationships with others, and
holistic and respectful change of the environment we share. And evolutionary
teaching must necessarily be critical.

Critique is nothing more or less than the process of discriminating between
'good' and 'bad' and of understanding how and why these arise. It is not itself
an act of improvement but it can be a preparation for improvement. At the least,
it can help us to deal better with an imperfect situation. This last point is true
whether we are reading a novel or making a political policy. There is nothing
necessarily subversive or carping about 'criticism'; criticism is about understanding a problem and solving it. A situation isn't 'a problem' until you find
something wrong with it. That is a part of criticism — finding something wrong
with a situation. But it is only a beginning. Unless you find something right with
it too, or at least something potentially right, there is no direction to go in to
solve the problem.

Sometimes this solution has to go well beyond the ingredients present in
the problem to begin with — sometimes we have to invent new ingredients to
solve problems, or redefine the problem so that it can be solved. Let me give
you an extended 'for instance'.

The approach adopted in this book has little in common with talk of education for 'a productive culture' or with prattle from ministers of education about
technical skills and export performance — with the whole sorry misinterpreta-
tion of human welfare that is most modern economics. However, paradoxically,
what is recommended here may well be more efficient at all of those things than
the approaches usually recommended, provided we redefine the problem. I think
I can safely boast that the approach adopted in this book is 'economically
unsound' if 'economically sound' means, as it usually does, something that

makes for continued and greater economic growth, defined as growth in Gross National (or Domestic) Product. The problem with economic growth as usually defined is that it doesn't put a price on air pollution and resulting rates of lung disease, except insofar as that raises the worker absentee rate. It is about growth in things that can be bought and sold, not things of value, like the beauty of a forest. The problem for economic growth is not that it is inherently wrong but that the whole world must soon stop having it, or, at least, having it in the form of the kind of goods we have been having. We don't know how long we have to change our ways, but the time scale is shortening as global pollution effects have now begun to show up in the air, the oceans and in the bodies of all living things.

Obviously, we can't give up our microwaves and cars overnight. But we should be educating for a transitional society. Children now entering our schools will not complete their secondary education until several years into the next millennium. We have to be future-directed. The urgent attention we now pay, in countries like the United Kingdom, the United States, Canada and Australia, to our fall from economic grace, the constant reading of the per capita income figures over the last hundred years, or yearning for the exchange rates of yesterday, are all backward-looking. Each of our countries must work out its own destiny and cope with its own fears of being economically outstripped by the rising economies of Asia, but it must also recognise that the old race for economic and military supremacy can only lead to collective disaster.

Take Australia. It is clear that it cannot hope to compete with cheap labour countries to its north and must seek its economic salvation in a combination of high value added (usually high technology) products and sophisticated services aimed at niche markets, and further processing of the raw materials (minerals and agricultural products) in which Australia enjoys a comparative advantage, plus perhaps some high capital industries where technology and a low proportion of costs in the form of labour might permit it to compete (steel). So far, the formula is the familiar one. Other countries will play their own variations of the themes. Britain, with few raw materials, will emphasise manufacturing and services more than, say, the USA, which has a significant resources sector.

But Australia has an advantage over northern hemisphere countries — space, and a relatively unpolluted environment. It can still preserve these things, *and* achieve some of the economic goals that seem so necessary to policy makers in the advanced societies in the transitional period to a sustainable world economy. The greatest niche market of all, and one that is uniquely suited to Australia's situation, is the development of less polluting methods of agriculture, energy generation, manufacturing, mining and the like. Research into these areas, and into energy conservation, plus incentives to industry to operate in a more sustainable way could generate patents on new processes which themselves would become exportable. In fact, developments of this kind could occur in all the advanced economies. And at the same time they can become models for the future highly developed but ecologically sustainable economies which the rising economies of Asia *must* themselves eventually become.

All of this involves changes. But not on a one-by-one basis: a configuration of interlocking changes is necessary. Without changed attitudes, changed laws, changed market conditions and changed technology the problem will not be solved but simply displaced. That is what has traditionally occurred. There was always more air, more space, more land, more economic growth. Polluting industries were simply put in remote areas, or exported to the Third World, effluent pumped further away, air pollution allowed to blow out to sea or onto our neighbours. Now we cannot any longer solve problems by pushing them away. Our problem-solving strategies must change. We now need co-operative (even universalised), holistic, problem-solving strategies, which involve the evolution of new ways of life.

What is Critical Theory?

Critical theory is a theory about rational problem solving which tries to open up the problem-solving process to just these kinds of new viewpoints and hence (potentially) new solutions. The problem with critical theory is that it is a highly esoteric, philosophically technical and, to the English-speaking world, foreign kind of theory. Unless we can find ways of making sense of it we run the risk of missing out on whatever it might be that critical theory can offer. The critical theory of education, developed largely in Germany since the Second World War,[2] tries to show how schooling can be educational in the fullest sense — in promoting the problem-solving power of learners in an evolutionary way. It has some connections with Marxism but, as many Marxists have said, has thrown out so much that Marxists usually consider essential, that it makes no sense to call it Marxist.[3] In many ways, it is close to Dewey's theory of education, but I believe it has developed a more useful account of educational actions and communication between teachers and learners than Dewey did. But like Dewey,[4] critical theorists consider democratic problem-solving methods to be the most efficient methods for communities to use in solving problems; like Dewey, they consider an open communication process to be essential to both community problem solving and to efficient development of the problem-solving powers of learners in classrooms. Unlike Dewey, the theory of critique, particularly as developed by Jurgen Habermas and those educationists who have drawn on his work,[5] provides the basis for a detailed analysis of actual examples of classroom interaction, an analysis which can identify communicative constraints on opportunities for enhancing the problem-solving power of learners. The theory of critique can provide the basis for a critical educational linguistics.

The development of this kind of linguistics has already begun. In *Language Policy Across the Curriculum* (Volume 1 of this series), David Corson uses critical ideas to put forward a model for democratic policy making at school level and shows how Habermas' ideal of open and uncoerced speech can help us think critically about communication in schools. As Corson points out, a useful point for a critical educational linguistics to begin is Habermas' critique of the theory of knowledge[6] and his attempt to define rationality and rational action in broader terms than the usual equation of those with science and technological action. Through Habermas' critique, which has evolved over the years and passed through several stages, we come to the conclusion that rationality is communicatively based and that action cannot be truly critical, and thus rational, if it is rational for only one individual or one nation.

Habermas' idea of knowledge has sometimes been described as a view of knowledge from the standpoint of sociology or history rather than philosophical epistemology. Perhaps a better way of thinking about it is to say that Habermas has come to believe that we, in the Western world anyway, have been asking the wrong question about knowledge; or rather, we have been asking our questions in the wrong order. We have been asking, as individual subjective consciousnesses: 'How can I know that something (e.g. a statement) is true?' Only then, when we have started to consider issues like evidence, the accuracy of the senses, objectivity and so on, have we asked how the society around us might influence our judgements. Habermas takes the view that the question we should start with is: 'How can members of a community come to an agreement that something is true?' and then, later, we look at how a community might come to feel that it has had a common experience, has experienced common evidence and so on. His answer to this question is couched in terms of a theory of communicative problem solving or action.[7]

Habermas initially focused his attention on the theory of knowledge because knowledge, particularly scientific knowledge, has become the basis of the most successful form of problem solving in human history — that based in technology. In this form of problem solving, improvement comes from a critique which shows that the knowledge-base of technology has limitations or that the technology which applies these principles has limitations.

The difficulty with scientific knowledge and the technology based on it has often been that the prestige of science has prevented effective criticism, especially if it came from non-experts. Habermas tackles the problem of critique at a meta-level. He criticises the idea of science that so insulates it from everyday life and from effective appraisal by democratic discussion. It is easy enough today to see how necessary Habermas' critique has been. We have seen Chernobyl and Three Mile Island, we hear every day about the side-effects of uncontrolled technology on the environment. Such criticism does not irrationally discard the achievements of science and technology but it does ask that we don't get lost in the trees for lack of a map of the woods.

Habermas' criticism of the prevailing view of scientific knowledge was that it was not only a narrow view of science but that it tended to assume that scientific knowledge was the only form of knowledge — ignoring linguistics, cultural knowledge and the like. He saw the obstacles to rationality as coming from many sources including the psychological depths of scientists' own personalities. He criticised the narrow view of science, without rejecting science as a whole, by looking at the social, historical and psychological situation of the scientist (and other knowers). The view that the obstacles to better (scientific) problem solving were largely of social, cultural and psychological origin led him to look more closely at the social interaction of scientists and specifically at their communication.

From the standpoint of education, rather than science, we are dealing with new learners rather than old learners, otherwise there is not much difference. New learners spend more time than old learners in discovering what old learners have already discovered; only as they become old learners can they begin to spend a great deal of time discovering quite new things. But even in looking at the discoveries in the past, new learners must develop their capacity as problem solvers — as discoverers. Otherwise, at the end of the formal schooling process, they will have had no practice in thinking for themselves — practice in rational inquiry. No, I wish to amend that statement. 'Thinking for themselves' is part of the problem. Somehow we must think for ourselves *and* be a part of a community of thinkers who help each other and check each others' tendencies to purely idiosyncratic or self-interested thinking.

'Instruction', which is the transmission of pre-decided chunks of old learning, may play a part in education, but evolutionary education must go beyond this if it is to prepare learners to solve new kinds of problems. The communicative process between teacher and learner must reflect this difference.

The Modern Educational Problem

However, widespread acceptance of the idea that schooling should be 'educational' is really a product of the modern world. Certainly, schooling has a long history but throughout most of that history it has been aimed simply at the replacement of the older generation with a mirror image of itself. The idea of 'education' also has a long history, but it is a history lived in the shadows, because 'education' contains the notion that the pupil can transcend the master — that the younger generation can go beyond the older — and this was not a widely accepted conception of the role of schooling, at least, not until the modern era. Even Socrates' vision of schooling looked backward to remembering a prior perfection in understanding and wisdom rather than forward to the radically new.[8] More Heraclitan visions were suppressed.

The idea that schooling should be educational was a seed which did not germinate until the collection of ideas, practices, laws, organisations, technologies and nation states we think of as 'modern Europe' fertilised it. The new way of life constructed by the European peoples between roughly 1700 and 1900 was called 'modern' for two reasons: the first, simply because it was recent, the latest, the modern; the second, because those who felt a need to name this era (in which they still lived) were deeply aware of the differences between their world and that of their medieval and post-medieval forebears.

The modernity of the new Europe was doubtless exaggerated. Later scholarship was to remind more recent generations of how great was the continuity of European culture with its past. But the very exaggeration, the exaltation of the new, is itself one of the defining characteristics of modernity. For modernity is a culture of the new, of 'progress' and the celebration of change. The central metaphors contain no images of a trickling increment of economic accumulation or gradual technical innovation; they are, instead, images of revolution (a wheel turned full circle). The very pillars of the old cosmos were pulled down and its patriarchal god expelled from the palace of human reason. Theology gave way to anthropology. The new liturgy was celebrated through the mechanical song of the loom and lathe, the new credo was the astronomical tables, the new vestments, the sober business suits of the cities. But the religious impulse survived in and beneath the new forms. The idea of human perfectibility did not vanish or remain confined to the surviving remnants of once universal traditional churches. It was transformed from a static looking heaven-ward to a dynamic, historical possibility. From its confinement to the biography of individuals it burst out into the world of human society and progress. It was transformed into the thinking of the new prophets of reason. The faith of these intellectuals in the possibilities of science and technology was matched only by their faith in the moral and political possibilities of human reason. These were to be realised through a democratic involvement in the processes of government by 'the people', and through the guidance of science applied to human affairs.

True, initially the reformers did not envisage mass political participation on the twentieth century model. The French Revolution was followed by an extension of the political franchise which reached only the propertied classes; the peasants were largely excluded. The role of education was confined to the preparation of these propertied classes for effective political participation. Similar limitations on access to education prevailed in England until the nineteenth century and even, for a time, in the USA. The inclusion of the masses in the democratic process more or less coincided with the extension to them of educational provision funded from taxes.

Kant expressed this modern faith and its belief in the possibilities of education in his treatise *On Education*:[9]

> it may be that education will be constantly improved, and that each succeeding generation will advance one step towards the perfecting of mankind ... It is only now that something may be done in this direction, since for the first time people have begun to judge rightly, and understand clearly, what actually belongs to a good education.

As we approach the new millennium, it is this faith in the possibilities of education and in its role in the evolution of human happiness that is at stake, along with the rest of the core of rational optimism that is at the heart of cultural modernity.

Modernity has been under attack from the beginning, but for two centuries or more these attacks made little impact. Many came from traditional sources, others, a very few others, from within. Today we are witness to new and more threatening external assaults from a reinvigorated 'traditionalism' — in the form of neo-conservatism — and to a threat from within in the form of a burgeoning self-doubt, now fully flowered into the funeral lily of post-modernism.[10]

Habermas acknowledges the one-sided and distorted self-understanding of modernity and shares much of the critique made by its opponents. But unlike either the neo-conservatives or the post-modernists, Habermas believes modernity may be reformed from within.[11]

Modernity created its own problems — through the hubris of an overconfident science and technology, through a failure to develop a level of social understanding commensurate with its technological power, through the overextension of bureaucratic power into everyday life and through the alienation of the self produced by a mass media intent on manipulation of identity. From a global perspective we can also see that modernity has taken on a specifically European form, and from a feminist perspective we can see the lineaments of patriarchal distortion as well. We must add these to the environmental problems which are, in a way, a result of these other distortions.

The four distortions must be overcome if the possibility of some preservation of the idea of reasonableness is to be rescued from itself.

Science developed a one-sided self-image which it then mistook for the image of all possible human knowledge. Innocent of an understanding of the social roots of inquiry, it became the captive of the strategic imperatives of government and the military/industrial complex. Technology was also misunderstood. It became a tyrant whose artificial life is sustained only by an unreflective amnesia concerning its origins in human social and cultural choice. Social science, borrowing these errors, has become a mere fool, prancing about in a farcical attempt to ape the 'hard' sciences' self-deception, instead of finding its own poetic. The logic of technology has permeated the products of government and more and more spheres of private meaning are being colonised by state functionaries in the name of efficiency. Over all this, like a hall of distorting mirrors in a Fun House, the mass media cast a net of reflections of what we are or might possibly become that successively aggrandises and maims us until all sensitivity is dead. Little wonder that angry voices call for either the illusion of the recovery of lost meanings, through the smashing of the mirrors, or for a carnival of the images in which the mirrors are re-arranged into an infinite regress of significations like the picture on the Quaker Oats package.

To all of this, Habermas proposes an educational solution, based on a transformation of the fundamental nature of our understanding of modernity. A book, like this one, that deals with classroom talk and its educational possibilities in a global context is not an accidental 'spin-off' from Habermas' critical project, but something which lies at the very centre of it. If the sickness that has gripped modernity could be summed up in one sentence it would be this: Modernity has forgotten the nature of the relationship between word, image, deed and community. It is through a re-theorising of the nature of the possibility for rational progress, based on a *communicative* understanding of rationality, in which rationality is brought into a balanced relationship with art, language and the bodily dimension of life, that Habermas seeks to rescue the modern, and education's role in the '... advance ... towards the perfection of mankind' of which Kant wrote.

Habermas' new, communicative understanding requires a complete reconstruction of earlier applications of his ideas by various educationists.[12] Habermas' early attempt to reform the theory of knowledge by criticising it from *within* — immanent critique — did not achieve all that he had hoped.[13] True, he made a useful case for the view that knowledge must be understood culturally and linguistically, rather than in the entirely artificial way that many philosophers of science had hitherto seen it. He pointed to the web of cultural and social relationships within which scientific activity was carried out and showed the artificiality of, on the one hand, admitting that scientific communities relied on 'conventions' of method to test theories or that their inquiries were carried out against a horizon of expectations which was socially created, and on the other, trying to build a wall between social and cultural life at large and the products of scientific activity. He argued that science should be seen as a part of society, like government or the legal system — it was one of the highest forms of inquiry, of sense-making by the human species — but it was still simply a human enterprise. The rest of social life influences it and, in turn, it has become one of the major cultural influences on the societies in which it has become institutionalised. But these arguments, although powerful, did not strike at the heart of the problem.

As mentioned earlier, when he realised that a change of perspective was required (a 'paradigm change'), he saw that the underlying question of all previous epistemology was only one of two possible questions. Instead of seeing knowledge in terms of a theory of the relationship between the consciousness of the individual and the method of inquiry, we might acknowledge that science is actually carried out not by separate individuals, but by communities. The way in which members of a community come to agree on the truth of a statement is no less important than the question of method. It strikes at the classical epistemological questions from a new angle. Instead of asking 'What methodological safeguards will let me be sure of the evidence of my senses?' we can ask: 'How is it possible for communities to agree on methodological rules?' The latter question is, in a sense, prior to the former, because it is only when there can be agreement that new knowledge becomes accepted as 'scientific'. The question of the agreement of a community, rather than the Cartesian question of the problem of certainty for an individual, is one that can be answered only through some sort of account of the discourse of that community. It thus produces a communicative account of knowing and coming to know (rational learning). We move from the scientist as romantic hero to the scientist as responsible member of a community. The gross and shameful parodies of this notion of social responsibility of science that characterised Stalinist regimes in eastern Europe should not blind us to the possibility of a legitimate understanding of social responsibility — responsibility to the community of inquiry itself: something many scientists under Stalin did not, perhaps could not, display.

From an educational point of view, this account points to a form of teaching and learning which is open to the discourse of inquiry — the continuing inquiry of the human species. Notice I did not say 'inquiry learning'. That phrase has a more specific meaning than 'open to inquiry'.[14] Learning which is open to inquiry need not waste a lot of time rediscovering phlogiston, the atom, evolution and so on. A scientist making a change of direction in research asks a colleague and gets a mini-lecture or goes to a library and 'reads up' the work needed. Then she goes on to inquire anew. In schooling, it follows that there will be a lot of instruction, lecturing, reading up and the like. After all, the children have to catch up on several thousand years of inquiry in a few. But open to inquiry means being aware of the processes that produced the knowledge, having *some* practice in open-ended inquiry for themselves, and/or awareness of the ongoing inquiry — the contemporary discourse — and some degree of access to that discourse. That means, of course, access to a community.

More specifically, open to inquiry means that theories and propositions entertained by students are entertained in such a way as to be open to the experience of the other as well as the self. Of course, there isn't time for all learning to be based on a full personal and critical review of the evidence or for a full sharing of experience with others. Much must be taken on faith. The crucial issue is the theory of inquiry that is used — the methodology the student comes to regard as normative. Unless students open out to others and to other cultures, they will be unable to undertake the evolutionary learning that the revision of their own cultural background will require, and without that, there will be no global solutions.

In this later work, Habermas distinguishes between critical theory proper — which is a theory of how the human species learns — and critique (including immanent critique and ideology critique). Critical theory proper is, in a sense, methodological. It is about our general capacity for critical discourse and rational problem solving and our nature as knowers. Critique is more specific; it can take many forms. It is a fallible, historically situated analysis of a particular set of relationships and how these stand in the way of more rational problem solving for the community of inquiry. One form it can take is ideology critique, which aims to identify the ideas and practices which prevent the emergence of clear understanding and more critical discourse.

Critical theorists have argued that one of the major sources of such ideas and practices lies in a particular way of understanding human knowledge. Standing squarely in the critical theory tradition, I will argue that many of the problems of teaching and learning in school classrooms flow from a fundamental confusion about the nature of knowledge and, in particular, of methodology. The dominant image of the method of inquiry in our classrooms is one which actually creates many of the problems which we are experiencing in our schools.

2 Context and Method

The Methodological Error of the Modern Curriculum

The modern curriculum fails because of its image of method. However, the word 'method', used in the context of schooling, is ambiguous. We are forced to ask: are we speaking of teaching method (pedagogy) or are we speaking of the method used by the original producers of the subject matter later incorporated in the curriculum (e.g. in the science curriculum, 'scientific method')? The answer to this question for the purposes of the present argument is 'both', *and* the relation between the two. However, for the sake of avoiding confusion I will call teaching method 'pedagogy'.

If we believe that the goals of education in schools should be evolutionary and the learning that takes place should be not only the basis of further inquiry but also itself open to inquiry, then the way in which learners come to know cannot be entirely separate from the way in which the human community at large comes to know. That is, pedagogy cannot be separated from method. There are several reasons for this inseparability. First, learners would be handicapped in further inquiry if the way they came to know was at odds with the way they would themselves eventually engage in inquiry. They would have to do a lot of unlearning. Second, even if the way they came to know was not at odds with later methods of inquiry, but was still not itself a process of inquiry, the habit of holding views on the basis of authority or faith would have to be overcome if further inquiry were to be efficient.

The process of inquiry in every area of human intellectual endeavour is becoming universalised. This process is most fully advanced in the natural sciences; there, one finds few barriers of culture or rationality in a relatively universal discourse of inquiry. In the more political sciences some significant barriers remain, but universalisation of the discourse is developing. Participation in a community of inquiry is more and more coming to mean a species-wide endeavour. The more knowledge is based on social influence, authority and power, the less likely it is to transcend the particulars of cultural and political location.

When new learners enter the discourse, they see the existing discourse as 'tradition', although it is actually developing and changing even as they learn.

The initial discourse of the learner is characterised by a strong emphasis on reception rather than challenge. But in a discourse that acknowledges its own historical relatedness and its constant development, there is always an element of dissonance. Harmony may be maintained only by learners finding a new voice, sounding new notes, since the harmony of discourse moves in a melodic development, rather than remaining confined to a single chord, endlessly repeated. And what is inquiry itself but a basic expression of human adaptability? The expression of oneself as knower and problem solver is as basic to the expression of life as such as any other expression of our powers, and is interwoven with art, love and self-expression.

One of the characteristics of the modern school's image of method — one of the mistakes endemic to modern educational thought and practice — is that it has a Cartesian self-understanding. Descartes begins his *Discourse on Method* thus:

> My present design, then, is not to teach the method which each ought to follow for the right conduct of his reason but solely to describe the way in which I have endeavoured to conduct my own.

But despite the modesty of his introductory remarks he nonetheless insists that he

> ... will not hesitate, however, to avow the belief that it has been my great good fortune to have very early in life fallen in with certain tracks which have conducted me to considerations and maxims, of which I have formed a method that gives me the means, as I think, of gradually augmenting my knowledge.

and later

> ... I continued to exercise myself in the method I had prescribed, for besides taking care in general to conduct all my thoughts according to its rules ... (I applied) the method in the solution of mathematical difficulties and even the solution ... of some questions belonging to other sciences.

He is sure that if others try his method, they will get similar results: 'I shall endeavour in this discourse to describe the paths I have followed ... in order that each one may be able to judge of them for himself.'

The full title of the discourse is instructive: 'Discourse on the Method of Rightly Conducting the Reason and Seeking Truth in the Sciences.'[1]

We can see in the foregoing extracts two key features of the Cartesian error: the belief that the truth is the product of a correct application of method rather than a product of discourse, and the belief that method is something that can be replicated by isolated, individual minds. The first belief is subtly undermined by Descartes' chosen title: *Discourse* on Method. If the method advocated in the discourse is *the* method, by what method did the discourse itself proceed? The second belief is given the lie by Descartes' act of publication of the book and by the rhetorical devices with which his discourse proceeds. If the method of doubt can nevertheless yield an incorrigible foundation for Descartes the individual, why does he appeal so often to *common* experience and suggest that the reader try it out for himself?

As Gadamer[2] has shown, truth and method do not stand in the relation to each other of product and process. If Gadamer is right in this respect, almost the whole of the modern approach to teaching method is wrong, but for reasons which are generally additional to those already adduced by opponents of product/process research on teaching and learning. There is no set of standardised procedures, no machinery for cranking out the truth. Learners cannot acquire true or warranted belief (knowledge) by the application of fixed rules, maxims, procedures or knowledge production processes, because, as several decades of critique have so clearly shown (Popper, Kuhn, Lakatos, Feyerabend, Rorty), this is not the way human communities of inquiry learn. Consequently, by applying fixed rules, procedures or processes, teachers cannot bring about learning — at least, not learning of the kind that is open to inquiry, or able to be described in terms of the attainment of warranted belief (knowledge).

Conversely, to the extent that teachers conceptualise the warranting of belief (coming to know) as the product of the employment of 'correct' methods of inquiry, whatever particular methods they may have in mind, they are making a mistake about the nature of knowledge which can only confuse and frustrate their pedagogical intentions (to the extent that this belief actually guides their pedagogy). We can find examples of this every day in the mathematics classroom, where pupils are contented with quite absurd results because they derived from the 'correct' method. Good maths students know that they need to use several methods as a check on each other and that some problems yield to no standard method but only to a unique mix of methods, guided by a mathematical imagination.

Teachers' Epistemologies

My own research[3] on secondary teachers' conceptions of knowledge shows that teachers display a range of views of the relation between knowledge and method. (This research has since been replicated several times.) Although evidence of this kind concerning views of teachers in countries other than Australia is limited, it appears to be consistent in broad outline with the Australian data.

The views of inquiry which teachers possess range across a spectrum of types. As Royce[4] first found, the notion of 'authority' as a source of knowledge is still a significant one, although the proportion of teachers who espouse recourse to authority as a central method of inquiry are few (outside some areas of curriculum such as religion or religious studies). More common is the operational understanding of inquiry, based on the notion of the sensory validation of logically articulated statements about named entities and their interrelationships, buttressed by a sense-based semantics for the naming of entities and interactions between them. This understanding of the truth–method relation is characteristic of logical empiricism in general and positivism in particular. Cruder versions of this view speak of 'scientific method' (in the singular). Such views are underpinned by an 'objective hermeneutics' — the view of the role of language in inquiry — that borrows the logical grammar of logical empiricism while replacing sensory observation with a more behavioural account of the basis of semantics, such as the account given by Quine's *Word and Object*. The problem for an objective hermeneutics is that it possesses little account of the truth of the referring functions of language and reduces meaning to a vehicle for logical-empirical knowledge rather than recognising overtly what it constantly relies on covertly — that logic and language involve their own form of hermeneutic knowledge. To put it crudely, if we know only through some kind of sensory warrant (or through some holistic balancing of a system of statements with sensory observation statements at the periphery), on what basis do we 'know' that any given logical connection in the system of statements is actually 'valid'? Is logical 'knowledge' — for example, the knowledge that a form of inference is valid — based (ultimately) on some kind of sensory warrant? Or are we dealing with two quite different senses of the word 'meaning', or perhaps, seeking to do away with it altogether?

A third understanding of inquiry is that of hermeneutics proper. In this view we can have knowledge of meaning that is either independent of the second kind of knowledge or, as in the views of some post-modernists, in some sense inclusive of it. The problem with this view is the problem of relativism. As a basis for pedagogy, it leads to a different teaching approach to logical empiricism, although it is prone to lapse into a covert authoritarianism which seeks to impose a given meaning system on student discourse.

But there is another category of teachers' conceptions of inquiry in which it is seen as some form of critical inquiry. Views of this kind were rare in the Australian data. In this view a kind of hermeneutic understanding is present, linked to some notion of the social character of inquiry, and the necessity for an understanding of the method of inquiry in terms of human conditions of the process of inquiry itself.

It is important to distinguish between teachers' espoused theories and their theories-in-use. Observations of teachers at work show a discrepancy between their espoused theory of inquiry and their teaching practice. It is also important to make a second distinction — between the *types* of view of inquiry which teachers manifested (as outlined above) and the view of any given teacher. Many teachers espoused several types of model of inquiry, each seen as appropriate in particular school subjects. These teachers were labelled 'Forms of Knowledge' teachers, following the terminology of Hirst and Peters. However, the critical view was absent from the list of forms recognised by these teachers.

In general, there was a high level of concord between the espoused view of inquiry and teachers' espoused views of pedagogy. But practices seemed to fall short of espoused views (as many teachers were aware) mainly by a falling away from ideals at the critical end of the spectrum. Teachers who espoused a critical view found themselves sometimes teaching from authority, or reduced to hermeneutic relativism, or, for the sake of simplicity, providing step by step methodological formulae for anxious students to follow. Teachers who viewed the knowledge in their field of learning hermeneutically (as pre-given systems of human meaning and culture) found themselves slipping back into either authoritarian privileging of one set of meanings over another or into forms of methodological objectivism.

The dominant view of knowledge of some teachers (mainly technology teachers) was of authoritatively given explanation and practices. The pedagogy was memorisation and imitation. These teachers emphasised the practical and saw knowing as knowing what was taught — essentially memorisation rather than understanding, practical or factual knowledge rather than 'theory'. This explains otherwise paradoxical statements such as: 'Basic science is very important whereas physics and chemistry aren't.'

One such teacher stressed that he tried not '... to be an authoritarian teacher ... to give them a fair amount of individual freedom provided they don't interfere too much with each other'; but he was not talking of freedom of inquiry, just freedom to get on with learning the canonical doctrine of the curriculum. Perhaps it is not surprising to find some of these teachers expressing views such as: 'I think that history and languages are of no importance to you whatever', and, from a high school teacher of technology: 'I would think basic mathematics [i.e. not theoretical but mensuration and arithmetic] is very very important and essential whereas a subject like psychology ... I think is of no real importance as a basic area of knowledge.'

The dominant view of knowledge on the part of teachers of science was logical-empiricist. The model of inquiry was of the warranting of statements by sensory observation. The typical pedagogy was the experimental testing of statements, observation of results and the falsification/verification of statements ('Aim: to test the hypothesis that …') or, in many cases, the induction of generalisations from observations of the behaviour of entities under experimental manipulation ('Aim: To observe what happens to the reagent when an acid is added'). This type of teacher is likely to talk about *the* scientific method. Theory is typically valued as well as facts: 'Factual knowledge would be just accumulated facts … I would define a model as an idea which encompasses all the facts and which is useful in predicting new facts.' The Cartesian certainty of these teachers is reflected in their confidence that the students should do lots of experimental work so that they can '… find out for themselves that it all works'. The view is summed up by the teacher who attributed the failures of technology to the fact that we haven't had enough of it yet. Another displayed a common view among this group. Only the 'hard sciences' are really knowledge:

> The discoveries of the physical sciences have been the most significant mainly because they have challenged the conventional wisdom and the church. However, the methods of science have been extrapolated to the social sciences and this seems to be largely invalid unless it is demonstratable in empirical terms.

I know what he means!

The dominant model of English teachers was hermeneutic. The model of critical method (in the literary sense) was the gradual discovery and construction of interpretations, often personal interpretations. The paradigmatic pedagogy was directed discussion and the study of model interpretations (e.g. teachers' or critics' interpretations).

However, the personal character of hermeneutic response was emphasised as against the social or cultural character of systems of meaning: 'The nature of knowledge is so difficult to define. There's certainly kids who'd know more about a particular topic than the teacher, because of their curiosity or their native ability …' But this knowledge is basically intuitive or personal:

> Because a person feels and knows it to be true it therefore has some objectivity … the appreciation of [school subjects] is basically intuitive especially when you get to things like the arts where aesthetic things are more obvious but even in the sciences the aesthetic is there.

The view of knowledge on the part of critical teachers (of various subjects, but most often humanities, social sciences or the arts) was that it was a collective product of a history of inquiry. The dominant model of method was that inquiry went beyond method to a sharing of experience and the construction of meanings and argument. This view also went beyond pedagogy — the control of children. The learning method appropriate was a flexible mix of access to diverse views, discussion, experiment and action — apprenticeship in participation. This view of knowledge is often expressed in complex ways and simple statements of it are rare. Here is one such statement:

> Perhaps even facts depend on the society and the person who's learned them ... What is a fact for one person, for one society, may not be a fact for another ... I believe that all people have an equal right to their own form of knowledge.

The forms of pedagogy displayed by teachers of various kinds range from acceptance of authority, followed by either memorisation or imitation, through the 'correct' application of a method, to the penetration/discovery of a meaning system and beyond, in rare instances, to the many-sided construction and reconstruction of the narratives of experience in an open-ended dialogue with other inquirers. (The acceptance of authority is not a form of inquiry, since the inquiry has already taken place elsewhere.) The application of fixed, canonical methods may be inquiry-oriented (as in 'guided-discovery instruction' in science classrooms), but the knowledge-product is regarded as gaining its authority from the method, to which appeal is had foundationally. The process of entering into a system of meaning, like learning a foreign (or ancient) language, is only inquisitive in a one-dimensional sense since there is a postulated 'given' system of meaning (of which the teacher is the master) and inquiry is limited to linguistic discovery procedures (Is that a grunt grunt? No, that is a bowwow!); of course, learning a system of meaning need not be like that. But then, the hermeneutics involved become critical hermeneutics and begin to connect up with the final category of the present analysis.

At the critical-hermeneutic level, the learning method becomes reflexive. The discussion of the adequacy or inadequacy of some system of meaning for providing an account of experience may now be opened up. The human conditions of the construction of narratives are effectively included in any account of the narrative. Such an approach could remain in a state of mutual incomprehension — and often does — but need not. But the emergence of any horizon-merging transcendence of difference is not a predictable or operationally producible outcome. Consensus emerges where it can, not necessarily where one may feel it is needed most. Only with the eyes of hindsight (as Lakatos[5] argues with regard to scientific progress) can we see the ontological ground upon which any emergent consensus was based — the grounds in our common humanity and the nature of the world. But such an openness is no more than a necessity in a species which learns about a universe whose nature it shares. We are not outside observers to a reality served under glass but participants in it, who pull our knowing selves up by the bootstraps of an as yet partially known nature of ourselves as knowers. And it is crucial to recognise that we do not do this simply as individuals.

Now, if the latter understanding of the nature of human inquiry is correct, the failure of the modern school may well have something to do with the fact that few teachers possess such an understanding and even fewer feel able to practise a pedagogy consistent with it — an 'erotetic'[6] pedagogy based on the learner's questions. But I want to do more than assert that an inadequate view of knowledge predominates in our schools or that teaching methods generally reflect this inadequate view. To take the next step in the argument I must give a more communicative account of schooling, focusing particularly on the nature of 'the context' of classroom communication.

Communication, Context and Praxis

Different understandings of learning are realised through different patterns of classroom communication. Patterns of communication in classrooms where teachers share the view that knowledge is a product of method, while displaying differences related to different views of methods (logical-empirical, hermeneutic), possess a common general structure which marks them off from critical teaching and learning. The crucial differences between 'method classrooms' and what I will call 'discourse classrooms' derive from different ways of relating what is said in classrooms and its context, and differences in the kinds of context/communication relationships constructed in classrooms and the nature of the knowing produced in them, particularly as that affects praxis.

The context-relatedness of teaching/learning communication is complex. Both communication (pedagogy) and methods of inquiry are context-related. To provide an extended example which will make these relationships visible, I will try to trace some of the connections from modern understandings of method in scientific knowledge, through understandings of methods *by* science learners, to pedagogical 'methods' of science teachers.

When we speak of the historical nature of inquiry we are referring, in part, to the fact that contexts change over time and with them, inquiry changes. One aspect of this change is generated by the emerging outcomes of inquiry itself. Each new discovery changes the baseline for future inquiry. This is true of communities of inquiry, such as physics or astronomy, but it is also true for individuals. The more we know, the more we can know. And inquiries are not carried on in total isolation from other changes and developments, or developments in other areas of inquiry. Wars and revolutions can speed up or slow down certain lines of inquiry. Politics influences lines of inquiry, through either funding changes or direct influence. In a similar way, the personal life of individual learners provides an environment for their learning. At one stage in a person's life they may be very interested in religious inquiry, at another in academic learning. During a personal crisis they may not be interested in deliberate inquiry at all, even though they may be learning a great deal.

But teachers frequently have a context-free understanding of learning or, at least, an impoverished notion of context. They tend to take little account of the dynamic character of context and its personal and actively constructed character, and even less account of the everyday knowledge pupils bring with them to the classroom, especially in highly structured subjects. Finally, in our teacher-dominated classrooms it is still the case that little account is taken of the context created by the co-presence of other learners. All of this is reflected in the communicative style of their teaching.

As Popper and Lakatos have shown, the changing context created in science by the flow of new ideas is like the horizon, viewed from the deck of a moving ship, ever changing but, apparently, still the same, until some new island looms into view. Beyond the horizon, as we look back, are the old, discarded theories, ahead are the new lands. The horizon ahead of us defines the present set of theoretical expectations and the problems that we can see now. But these, in their turn, will be discarded and forgotten.

Difficult to live in such a Heraclitan world! So most scientists don't. They adopt a convenient objectivism, seeing the world as if the present circle of our vision were a permanent and complete vision of reality, and the meanings of scientific concepts were as fixed as the deck fittings on the ship, rather than flowing like waves beneath its keel. To add a final twist to our analogy of the ship, and make many scientists more anxious, the ship is really a ghostly structure that is dissolving even as we speak, and being rebuilt just as fast as it breaks up, even as we sail on in it.

The objectivism of many scientists may be a useful fiction, and supportive of certain kinds of research, but it tends to dominate the school curriculum in association with an erroneous concept of learning. But fashions in educational thinking change. We are now moving out of the objectivist period and its associated theory of learning, that is as the acquisition of fixed conceptual structures through the effect of graduated rewards and punishments. There has been an increased recognition of the active, cognitive character of high order learning. Recent discussions of science teaching display this new, more dynamic awareness.

The Co-construction of Cognitive Context

The emphasis in recent cognitive psychology of learning, as summarised by West and Pines in respect of science teaching, is on the interplay between 'intuitive knowledge' and the formal knowledge taught in the school. This intuitive knowledge is described as the 'sense making' that we all develop from language, culture and interaction. It is often haphazard, and acquired over a long time. It is also often almost subliminal and so accepted that it is simply the way things are. Educational psychology, I want you to meet Phenomenology! This is the everyday or common-sense knowledge of which phenomenologists have spoken for so long. It is now recognised by educational psychology, although long asserted by phenomenology of education, that the formal knowledge of the school: '... is someone else's interpretation of the world, someone else's reality. Its primary characteristic is authority. It is 'correct'; it is what the book says; what the teacher says.'[7]

If this new knowledge is not integrated with the old, it cannot draw on the virtues of everyday knowledge. Everyday knowledge works; it is speedy, usable, widely integrated. The new knowledge is unfamiliar and uncertain. It is expressed differently from common sense. It doesn't connect up with the rich mass of existing ideas and experiences. Only when it is integrated with everyday knowledge, and everyday knowledge changed to permit this, does it become easy to use outside the classroom-type situations in which it is first encountered.

A range of responses to the new knowledge is possible. It may match the old quite closely, in which case it is easily assimilated. It may challenge the old, which creates a need to resolve contradictions. Or there may be no old knowledge of the kind that is being encountered. A possible strategy in all cases is to treat the new as if it is something quite different from everything we actually believe and base our actions on. This is cognitive apartheid. Obviously, this is likely to be more common if the new challenges the old.

Under such circumstances, it is difficult for the new knowledge to be really made the pupil's own, a part of their reality. It gets learned in a shallow way, and, as research shows, is quickly forgotten after the last examination, if it was ever really understood in the first place:

> ... genuine conceptual learning occurs when learners make their own sense of (new) knowledge. [But] ... the curricula of schools are other people's knowledge, imposed (with the power of authority) on the student. Not surprisingly, some students do not bother to make personal sense of this knowledge but merely play the school 'game' of rote learning and reproducing the curriculum knowledge.[8]

However, a critical approach goes a little further than the cognitive constructivism which cognitive psychology has only so recently attained. Constructivists like West and Pines still conceptualise the emotional dimension in knowing in a passive, *ad hoc* way. Concepts like 'ownership' and 'authority' do not indicate the integrated nature of knowing. As we will see below, knowing *is* a commitment or claim, not something separate from the feelings of the knower, but a way of feeling in its own right.

The history of cognitive theories of learning has been an interesting one, and can be correlated quite closely with the ages of teachers, which in turn indicate which kind of theory may have prevailed at the time they were trained. In the beginning, as Perkins and Salomon[9] have recently argued, I.Q. researchers argued for a general kind of ability which could transfer across tasks. Other notions of general cognitive skills followed. This gradually gave way to a body of research in the 1960s and 1970s that cast doubt on the transfer of general cognitive skills. Only recently have we begun to understand the rather special conditions under which such transferable skills might operate: it is possible under conditions where 'local' and general skills can interact. And here's the rub: most classrooms do not offer such conditions. The formal curriculum has no real role for the pupil's personal reality. There is little space in classroom processes for pupils to take the time or command the resources to question the incoming abstract curriculum knowledge. This would require an interaction pattern which respects the child's naive, but real-for-her view of, say, physical processes, and allows the child to bring this into interaction with the incoming views from the community of inquiry of the physical sciences.

Brown, Collins and Duguid[10] see concepts as tools:

Because tools and the way they are used reflect the particular accumulated insights of communities, it is not possible to use a tool appropriately without understanding the community or culture in which it is used.

Conceptual tools similarly reflect the cumulative wisdom of the culture in which they are used. Their meaning is not invariant but a product of negotiation within the community ... Teaching methods often try to impart abstract concepts as fixed, well-defined, independent entities that can be explored in prototypical examples and textbook exercises ... communities of practitioners are connected ... by intricate, socially constructed webs of belief ... To learn to use tools as practitioners use them, a student ... must enter that community ...

In these terms, much school work is inauthentic. It is characterised by well-known absurdities, such as teaching formal grammatical systems when the aim is to get students to use language in ways considered grammatically correct, a different task altogether. But the contexts of real activities are rich and complex;

the impoverished contexts of the classroom are faced by the problem that we do not know which features of context are essential to a community and which can be simplified away.

Where it is recognised by teachers and curriculum makers that the knowledge of physics is itself a changing product of continuing conversation, including conversation about evidence, argument and experience, it is much easier for teachers to respect the child's view, and allow time for the child to engage with the counter-commonsensical ideas of the physicists.

In the method classroom, knowledge is seen as a surefire product of 'correct' rituals of *the* scientific method. The common-sense ideas of pupils are simply pushed aside. They aren't even there (pedagogically). The slate isn't so much wiped clean as written over. But children do not come as *tabula rasa* to be written on at will in the language of immortal concepts that will stand them in good stead for life. They come as active co-creators of the communicative context which is itself the inferential basis for understanding or misunderstanding the teacher's utterances. This complex, fluid reality must be recognised for truly evolutionary teaching to happen.

Something of the possibilities is captured by Max Miller's conception of collective learning.[11] Miller observed children discussing moral dilemmas in groups. He showed how they co-operated in resolving the dilemmas and how the contribution of each child was related to her cognitive developmental level. But more than that, he showed the way children a little further along the developmental path than others played a significant role in moving the discourse of the whole group to a higher developmental level. These children were the sceptics. They raised difficulties. They insisted on making sense for themselves and in so doing helped the whole group make better sense.

The work of Pontecorvo and others in Italy and France on group discussion and the acquisition of both literacy and scientific concepts reveals a similar process in the domain of cognitive development. Pontecorvo focuses on the social facilitation of knowledge acquisition and the roles different group members play in problem-solving dialogue:

> ... complex processes of 'discourse-reasoning' were found to occur both during convergence between speakers' points of view and during disagreements and quarrels. While during 'co-construction' phases, to use Damon's term, the children are piecing the various incomplete parts of their ideas together, during the debating phases, their reasoning around the problem proceeds vigorously, by means of disagreement with statements made by others, justification of one's own point of view, counter arguments, and attempts to find ... more satisfactory guarantees and backings.[12]

Later work[13] revealed the important part played by one kind of participation in such dialogues — the role of the sceptic. As was the case in Miller's study, sceptical participation was often the catalyst for a stage-transcending movement in the cognitive level of group discussion. For stage-transcending learning, opposition rather than agreement was definitive. This suggests, yet again, that children may well learn more quickly when they have room, as Habermas would say, for agreeing, disagreeing or seeking more information about the claims advanced by others, including teachers.

The interactional dimension of inquiry calls forth a recognition of our mutual contribution to and hence our mutual responsibility for inquiry. It requires us, too, to recognise the limits of cognitive and pedagogical individualism. In this way, it provides a counterbalance to the excessive romanticism and individualism of the dominant Western images of 'the scientist' as intellectual knight errant.

However, there is another set of implications which are more decisive for our present purpose. Individualism is not simply an epistemological mistake in the theory of inquiry, it is an attitude adopted by inquirers first of all towards themselves, and then towards others. When our relationship with others is not anchored in a recognition of our mutual responsibility for learning, but in a sense of competition and separation, we dehumanise ourselves. What may initially begin as a methodological prescription can easily become an existential attitude. Something of the sort happened to behaviourism.

Of People as 'Learning Things'

Initially, behaviourism was a methodological prescription. Its rationale was based not on a mechanistic view of human functions but on a methodological view that we could make *reliable* observations only of external behaviours rather than of inner thoughts and feelings. There was no suggestion that people did not have such things, or that they should be treated as if they had not. The purpose of the prescription was scientific, not practical. Somehow, several decades later this led to a technology in which it was suggested that the whole of society should be run on the basis of manipulating people by a series of rewards and punishments (Skinner's *Walden II*). A scientific strategy had become a political strategy. A way of studying human beings had become a way of dealing with them as if they were non-thinking things, rather than potential fellow inquirers.

From a methodological prescription for researchers studying learning — studying it as a change in external, observable *behaviour* brought about by changes in the environment (experience) — we eventually derived a method of pedagogy which rested on the principle that you should teach as if your aim was to change a pupil's behaviour, not the contents of her thoughts, her character, or her feelings. This was ignored methodologically because inferences concerning these are precarious for given individuals. For the purposes of research, the aspects of an individual essential to treating them like a person — someone with an 'inside' like us — were treated like an electronic 'black box', a gadget we plug in and hope will work. Almost from the beginning, the researchers were forced to ignore their own prohibition, and postulate entities like intentions or thoughts, so it wasn't so much of a disaster for research, although it undoubtedly delayed progress in cognitive science for decades. However, it was a disaster for theories of pedagogy. Teachers were asked to operate on the manipulation of pupil behaviours by rewards, and to take the production of specifiable behavioural performances as evidence of learning. Not only do such strategies fail with most learners, as we will see in the next chapter, they also exert a negative motivational influence.

In his famous essay, 'Education after Auschwitz', the early critical theorist Adorno insisted that Auschwitz was made possible by a view of human action in which '... men become the kind of person who make themselves in some degree the same as a thing. "Then," he says, "if it is possible, they make others into things, too".'[14]

We are entitled to ask of any view of human learning and inquiry: 'What image of humanity is inherent in it?' and 'How do learners fit into this idea of inquiry?' In short, in any theory of teaching and learning there is an imbedded view of the relationship between teachers and learners. Do they relate like things or like people? Do they share a common responsibility for inquiry or do those who have already learned something treat new learners as if they were things to be manipulated into learning? Do we as educators seek to create 'true belief' or 'true believers'?

Questions about the kind of creatures we see ourselves as dealing with are *ontological* questions — questions about the ontological presuppositions of teachers and learners about each other and about inquiry itself.

3 Ontology and Action

The Way We See the World

Let me be quite frank. The argument I present in this chapter is complex and in some places uses unfamiliar ideas. I think you will find that the effort to understand it is worthwhile, and it is necessary to do so to get the full benefit of the more practical sections of the book.

In their phenomenologically influenced discussion of the teaching/learning relationship, Scudder and Mickunas[1] develop an account of education in terms of dialogue, language and enculturation, that shares much in common with the approach adopted here. Although they do not pay explicit attention to the ontological questions that this chapter will deal with, their treatment of the teacher/learner relationship as an I/Thou relationship has much the same sort of implications as those discussed above. They also emphasise the fact that the foundations of educative experience are found in the everyday world of children and teachers, because it is only there that really meaningful involvement is found. In the meanings of daily life we find the roots of motivation and action and hence all that is practical and effective. Meaning is rooted in everyday language and experience and motivation in everyday action. In turn, these are sedimented into 'orientations' or schemata, which are stores of commitments, dispositions and beliefs. New, abstract and formal knowledge, and dispositions associated with it, make little impact on the learner if not deeply intertwined with everyday realities. Education is an enculturation process — a moving into a way of life. Its medium is language and experience, its method dialogue and its product, culture. It succeeds only when a student's *life* changes, rather than only a small corner of the mind. This is both a frightening and a noble conception of the responsibility of teachers. It is also why the role of the sceptic is so important. The sceptic is the person who says, 'Yes, but ...' and it is that 'but', embodied in a person in relation to others, which forces the restructuring of the existing schemata so necessary if learning is to go beyond mere surface acceptance of new ideas to genuinely usable problem solving of a new kind. The sceptic is not simply someone who disagrees. That is why sceptics are so annoying, and why in less humane societies than ours they have often been put to death. A sceptic is someone who has the courage to *withhold* acceptance. There can be many reasons for this, not all of them creditable, but when sceptics withhold acceptance of a generally held idea because it doesn't fit their own experience, their scepticism can be very productive.

Scudder and Mickunas set their account in the philosophy of Martin Buber. Buber's 'I–Thou' relationship, the basic *human* relationship we first learn when we begin to differentiate ourselves from our mothers, is extended in the case of education to an 'I–Thou–It' triad — I and Thou in dialogue about the It, the subject matter.

The value of a phenomenological element in human studies is quite simple. Setting aside the question of truth or correspondence with reality, the study of phenomena (things as they appear to us) is a study of *how* we perceive, rather than of whether what we perceive is real. By setting aside or bracketing the reality question we can study the structure of our ways of thinking about our experience. This study shows that our way of seeing the world is influenced by something other than 'the way the world really is', by our emotions, intentions and purposes — our 'attitude to existence'. In this way we can identify quite basic categories, learned in infancy, which we use and re-use to organise our later thinking about the world. These categories form the structural building blocks of our thinking — self, other, inner, outer, things, persons, natural, artificial, animal, human, and so on.

The basis of the argument I wish to make in the present work is also phenomenological, but it is not necessary to go to Buber for it. Habermas draws on the same general insights of phenomenology that Buber used to distinguish between the participatory attitude, which is that of a person among persons, and the objectivating attitude, which is the attitude we direct towards things.

The idea of a 'personal' relationship does not require any notion of intimacy, of getting 'personal'. There can be considerable social distance involved. Enemies can take things 'personally'. What is at stake is the way we treat another person — as a thinking, feeling, meaning being like ourselves, or as a thing. Do we argue, love, and seek to understand or do we manipulate through the appearance of these things (or simple force)? The 'way we treat' here includes the way we use language. Dialogue isn't simply talking to someone, it is talking to them as if they were thinking, feeling beings like ourselves, rather than voice-activated robots.

Habermas' account allows us to explore the nature of the assumptions we make about those we talk to, how this relates to the motivated, meaningful deeds we perform within a culture (actions), the background knowledge of interlocutors and the implications of this for the possibility of enculturation into universal forms of rational inquiry. As this account develops we also come across the roots of critique.

Habermas' Communicative Development

Since his inaugural professorial lecture at Frankfurt in 1967,[2] Habermas has been committed to a revision of social thought and practice through a reformulation of the theory of knowledge. His first attempts to do this pictured science as something society produced in the same way as culture. In essence this project is the same as Dewey's project of 'epistemology naturalised' — knowledge as something an intelligent species produces. The key problem for Habermas' version of this project, as so much of the secondary literature also testifies,[3] is that of the link between rationality and the moral and practical issues which arise in social life. This problem arose because the modern understanding of knowledge grew up through a long struggle between science, theology and politics and the growth of science at that time required a strict separation of facts from values and religious beliefs. But what may have been necessary then has become a burden today. We may never seek to run facts and values together as once was done, but we need to bring them into a productive relationship, if we still hope for a more humane technology and a more rational politics.

Habermas' attempt to tackle these issues in *Knowledge and Human Interests* employed the method of immanent critique of the epistemological assumptions of pragmatism, empiricism, positivism and Marxism. In that book, Habermas identified three forms of knowledge-producing purposes or interests:

1.   an interest in control, associated with a positivist self-understanding of the sciences and with the world of work;
2.   an interest in understanding, associated with the hermeneutic sciences and cultural processes;
3.   and an interest in emancipation, associated with the critical sciences and progressive social evolution. Critical science included and completed the other two.

This trichotomy has been employed quite widely in educational theory.[4] It has also been quite widely misunderstood. The three interests are not separate in fact but only analytically. They are co-present in each and every human action. The critical interest is not incompatible with the other two, and they complement each other.

However, the response to Habermas' strategy of interest-based critique of knowledge, even from sympathetic critics, was not encouraging. These responses are summarised in Thompson and Held's *Habermas: Critical Debates* (1982). Habermas' 'Reply to his Critics' in that volume foreshadowed a different approach to the problem.

From Epistemology to Ontology

Habermas sets out his reasons for the paradigm change. He does this in the form of reflections on the failure of Adorno and Horkheimer's critique of scientism. This critique proceeded immanently; but the path of immanent critique is a 'rocky path',[5] as Habermas himself found out, because it works only within the philosophical position under criticism, and thus, within its limitations: in this case, from within the philosophy of traditional systematic epistemology which has 'outlived its own claims'.[6] All that immanent critique can do is demonstrate the inadequacies of the view being criticised. It can't provide a positive indication of some better view. In the case of epistemology, this critique demonstrates the inadequacy of the conceptualisation of epistemology as *the* fundamental form of philosophy, since all epistemologies rest on some account of the nature of knowers. Epistemology is oriented towards method, towards accounts of how we can reliably know, but method is secondary, not primary, for how we can come to know is always subject to the context of the history and place of inquiry and to the nature of knowers. We must first ask who it is that knows. A phenomenology of knowledge may tell us something about our style of knowing in a very general way, but actual historical examples of knowledge, such as Newton's theory of gravitation, can only be understood in a concrete historical context. What stage had this area of thought reached before Newton? What equipment or technology did Newton have that helped him develop his theory? What discussions took place at the time which influenced his thinking and speeded up or slowed down the acceptance of his ideas?

Habermas argues that when traditional systematic epistemology seeks to address its classical and central question — How can I warrant the truth of a statement/proposition? — it not only makes phenomenological assumptions, it also makes a number of ontological assumptions about the knowing subject and his or her consciousness. Habermas uncovers the ontological assumptions implicit in one well-known epistemology — Popper's 'three worlds' view of knowledge.[7] The essence of Habermas' argument is that the epistemologist must assume a world of common physical objects, of decision-making systems, of social structures and above all, of intersubjectivity. It is not sufficient, as Popper does, to say that all that is the business of the 'sociology of knowledge'; these things are inextricably linked to the most fundamental issues concerning the

identity of the experiences/phenomena with which rival scientific theories or different observers might be said to deal, a point we will come back to below. If
you leave the concrete reality of knowers out of the picture you create a circularity. Only the relative success and prestige of the natural sciences has permitted this question to be ignored. In the social sciences the circle is much smaller.
Instead of getting out of the circle by denying subjectivity, Habermas gets out of
it by affirming it and including the species' knowledge-forming activities within
the whole history of the species. Knowledge and the evolution of knowledge is
part of our history as a species. Social ontology is prior to epistemology.

Habermas turns to an exploration of the ontological assumptions of particular epistemologies — what kind of humanity do they presuppose? As discussed
in Chapter 1, the new starting point is: 'How can two or more people agree on
the validity of a warrant for the truth of a statement?' or 'Who is it that seeks to
know?' Epistemological questions are then set *within* a theory of knowers as
communicative beings set in society and history. The heart of this theory is a
theory of social, that is, communicative action, and the relationship between
validity judgements and the interpretation of the meaning of utterances. In
agreement of a sort with Foucault, Habermas is arguing that the social structure
gets 'inside' the concepts, methodological standards and theories of science. For
education, this requires a parallel shift: from the focus on the educational implications of epistemological positions which has dominated the work of many previous theorists, such as Scheffler, to a focus on the epistemic politics of the
knowing community — who is doing the discovering and whose knowledge is
it, anyway? It is true to say that teachers' epistemologies are reflected in their
pedagogy and curricula, but we need to recognise that the epistemologies have
not descended immaculately from heaven. People, even scientists, take up particular ways of seeing their science because they like them, they maybe agree
with their deeper intuitions about the nature of things, or a powerful patron likes
them, and so on.

Habermas is not arguing that scientists cheat on their data, or that given
certain assumptions their experiments don't work out the way they are reported
to do. But he is saying that many of the decisions scientists have to make as scientists are not able to be routinised, put into an algorithm, and made totally
rational and transparent. Choosing between rival theories is essentially a matter
of making a jump in the dark, no matter what evidence has accumulated. You
can test rival theories, but if they are theories of any scope the assumptions you
need to make to test them will not be independent of the theories themselves.
You can accumulate falsifications and corroborations as the theories fail or pass
tests. But any theory of scope has a very, very large class of non-trivial implications, and at any given stage of historical development we will have tested only
a few of these and those we have tested will have been chosen in various ways,

some influenced by our deeper intuitions and epistemological commitments. If the set of tested consequences of a theory at time 1 should favour theory A, that is no guarantee that at time 2 a larger set will do so. There is no guarantee in the Popperian approach against a politics of such choices. Whatever the account you try to give, it will rest on the knowing being done by real people making commitments that can't ever be totally and fully justified.

So it is not enough to develop a social-pragmatic epistemology and apply it to education, which was Dewey's strategy in *Democracy and Education*. That is only a half-way house. Certainly, it avoids the problem of epistemology, by moving away from traditional views to an epistemic stance which sees inquiry as a free-floating activity of the species, anchored only in circumstances and the current level of development, but it does this somewhat abstractly. It does not come fully to grips with the social-reflexive dimension — what sort of knowers are pragmatic knowers? If they must be open-minded, freely communicating members of a community of inquiry, as Dewey asserts they must be, doesn't this constitute the essential condition of their inquiry rather than a supposed cognitive commitment to pragmatism? A full-blooded *reflexive* application of Dewey's own 'biological-anthropological method' leads to a shift in the theoretical centre of gravity. It is a shift at several levels, not just at the level of the theory of knowledge. The new critical theory is 'reconstructive science' — an anthropological science of our being as knowers.[8] Critique itself is now not an application of epistemologic rules, but a process based on a 'biological-anthropological' theory of critique, resting directly on an ontology of communities of inquiry and the interpretation of meaning in them. This points to basing critique on overcoming the sources of limitation and bias within such communities and on an understanding of how they create new meanings — how they *learn*.

Collective Learning and Utterance Meaning

It is important to understand some of the technicalities of Habermas' new theory of meaning because they are directly applicable to the analysis of the communication and meaning-making of teachers and learners.[9]

The key to Habermas' latest ideas about meaning is a new connection he makes between the truth or moral validity of a statement (or action) and its meaning. He argues that participants in a process of communication are unable to understand meaning objectivistically without, at the same time, ceasing to view actions from a participant's standpoint. That is, there is a fundamental difference in phenomenological attitude between observers and participants.[10] As a participant, the conditions of understanding are such that you are simultaneously and jointly oriented to several dimensions of meaning in communication, not just one. The objectifying observer (e.g. the behavioural observer) can stand outside the community of interpretation, but the price is a lack of understanding of the multiple and interrelated layers of meaning, and a falsification of the way the knowing process is understood by the knowers themselves.

Habermas asserts that understanding meaning in this deep sense also requires an understanding of the ontological and moral/practical presuppositions of an utterance and that this understanding is only complete when some position is taken on the validity of these. He sketches an argument as follows:

> The interpreter observes under what conditions symbolic expressions are accepted as valid [or] rejected; he notices when the action plans of participants are coordinated through consensus formation and when the connections among the actions of different agents falls apart due to lack of consensus. Thus the interpreter cannot become clear about the semantic content of an expression independently of the action contexts in which the participants react with a 'yes', a 'no' or an abstention. And he does not understand these yes/no positions if he cannot make clear to himself the implicit reasons that move the participants to take the positions they do … reasons form the axis around which processes of understanding revolve. But if, in order to understand an expression, the interpreter must *bring to mind the reasons* with which a speaker would … defend its validity, he is himself drawn into the process of assessing validity claims. For reasons are of such a nature that they cannot be described in the attitude of a third person, that is, without reactions of affirmation or negation or abstention.[11]

Let me put this argument in the form of a simple example. A hearer is spoken to in church by the person sitting next to them about, say, a sexual matter. The hearer's knowledge of the culture and its rules about appropriate venues for speaking about certain topics may permit interpretation of the intent of the speaker in several ways. If the hypothesis that the speaker is culturally or linguistically incompetent is set aside, the hearer cannot avoid an interpretation in which the knowledge that the speaker is 'breaking the rules' is taken into account. To interpret talk successfully in a culture you need to 'know' the rules and what counts as following a rule, but if you do, you will, *in* the act of interpretation, form a judgement about whether the speaker is speaking in a culturally appropriate way or not. The general background claim of speakers — that they are speaking in a normatively appropriate way — would, in this case, have to be rejected.

One mistake commonly made by critics of Habermas at this point is to assert that they can imagine an observer who doesn't react in the attitude of a participant, but merely 'notes' the meanings without judging their validity.[12] I think what I have said above is enough to indicate that 'noting' also involves an incipient judgement about whether or not an action (e.g. an utterance) is normatively valid or not. One can note the semantic meaning of a word by finding it in a dictionary, but that finding will inevitably reveal whether or not the way it was used seems to have been in accordance with its dictionary meaning or not. Much the same might be said of understanding what sort of interpersonal claim an utterance is making against the 'dictionary' of the norms of a culture for a given situation. To refuse to respond to the validity claim in an utterance is always possible, but merely to note it is not the same thing as understanding it, or rather, the 'it' that is noted is not the full meaning of the utterance, only its semantic or 'logical' meaning. We see this distinction between mere semantic meaning and a broader conception of meaning when someone makes a remark that we consider insulting or 'out of place' and they say, disingenuously, and in a different 'way', and in a now different context, 'But I only said ... [semantic meaning of words] ... Why should anyone take offence?'

What the critics fail to see at this point is that Habermas is not talking about his special sense of 'discourse' here, but about everyday communication, where culture (beliefs, norms) is shared and in which, as most commentators agree, participants are normally oriented to each other as truth-telling, appropriately speaking, sincere communicators.[13] When discourse emerges, it is because norms have broken down, old truths have come into question, and so on. Then the whole tenor of communication is addressed to questions of *standards* of validity and problems of how to judge it, and it is even more difficult to deny that participants in this kind of talk are understanding utterances as argumentative commitments (or claims) to which others are required to react,[14] or that the meaning of an utterance in a discourse situation is precisely a commitment/claim and can only be understood by being aware *inter alia* of its conformity/non-conformity with participants' 'stores of commitments' and with commitments already announced in the talk.

Of course, it is possible for an observer to take an objectifying attitude to the utterances of another, but only by 'bracketing' the meaning of them, in the manner, say, of early behaviourism. This results in a loss of meaning. A teaching action which ostensibly raises validity questions, as all teaching actions oriented to knowledge must do, but which is pursued on the basis of a strategy constructed from a viewpoint which takes no account of anything but the learner's external behavioural conformity in the production of 'correct' performances under test conditions, provides no room for learners to respond rationally to the claims advanced. It also leads to a form of communication where teachers simply miss student meanings altogether. Sometimes teachers treat students as if they couldn't possibly be interested in seeking to understand a knowledge claim and the evidence and arguments for it, and relating this to existing everyday knowledge and experience, to all that is real and meaningful in their lives. They are seen as individuals who must simply be made to reproduce the point of view being advanced, by whatever means seem expedient and economical. This is already well on the way to treating students like things. In this case, not a robot, but a special kind of thing — a human thing — a manipulable bundle of nerve ends and stored ideas.

An extension of this argument, of which more below, is provided by Perry's (1988) distinction between the 'proposition created by an utterance' and the proposition *expressed in* an utterance. For instance, when a person makes a statement, you can derive an imbedded proposition from it — 'that X'. But this proposition can be imbedded in many ways of speaking, for example, 'We may have to be prepared for the possibility that X ...' If the statement 'that X' is uttered in a context of argument where it is taken as an assertion we get a second proposition: 'I assert "that X".' In a context, single propositions are seen as relevant and as having 'status' in an argument. However we attempt to formally represent this status, or whether we agree with Perry's way of doing it or not, it is certainly an additional dimension of meaning. It is difficult for a learner who is not permitted speaking moves of the kind which can reflect on the direction of an argument to respond to that aspect of propositional meaning *created by* teacher utterances, such as might be involved in a line of questioning, and hence to respond to validity claims inherent in the role an individual propositional claim plays in a wider strategy of argument. Students must find *the problem* valid or meaningful as well as the separate steps towards its solution, or, at the least, understand the individual propositions in an argument *as parts of an argument* against some general background awareness of what-it-is-all-for.

The crucial point here is Habermas' insistence on a human ontology for the reasoning process. There is no abstract ontological location where reasons or lines of reasoning can exist independently of human purposes and relationships. Reasons are something that human beings do not simply 'have' — they *advance* them. And what is more, they advance them in some context of intellectual or practical problem solving. That is, they have reasons for having reasons! The technical point we can derive from modern logic, that the process of scientific reasoning cannot be formally represented without loss and that judgements themselves cannot be wholly formalised, is only a negative way of saying that meaning is a real thing that real people *do*. Arguments cannot be understood in a purely formal way or from what Hamblin calls a 'god's eye view'. Arguments are a way of acting. At issue is the question of the ontological commitments not of epistemological theories, not even of theories of inquiry, but of inquiries themselves. Are students participating *as* interlocutors — thinking dialogue partners? If they are not, how can the arguments they deal with come to *belong* to them, and so move (motivate) them and be used by them to move the world?

Habermas insists that when one understands a reason one cannot avoid taking a position on it, because to understand a reason is to be far enough immersed in the community concerned already to have a great deal of experience, commitment and evidence about the bases of the reasoning of that community. It is not normally possible to partition ourselves cognitively and emotionally in such a way as to insulate this commitment when interpreting the reasons participants give for their actions.

One of the implications of Habermas' thesis is interesting in what it suggests for the politics of social research. In many forms of social analysis, the social scientific observer claims some epistemic privilege for his or her observational position. This is necessary if the subjects of research are to be seen in an objectivating attitude. However, it is not often recognised that this is achieved only at the expense of ontologically dehumanising the research subjects by adopting a simpler set of ontological presuppositions to describe their world(s) than is assumed to apply to the observer's own. This applies to teachers too. The scientific observer's epistemically privileged position is similar to the teacher's privileged knowledge, which turns into a cognitively significant interactional advantage, to which learners cannot rationally respond, because their relationship with the teacher and success in school is defined in terms of accepting and reproducing the teacher's views. Looked at linguistically, interpretation is radically dependent on context, and the ontological assumptions of speakers and hearers about each other are a part of that context. Asymmetries in these assumptions create communication problems because they result in interpreters working from different (perceived) physical and social realities. This creates validity problems, because it means some members of the community of inquiry will be assenting to claims on bases other than belief that the arguments supporting them are good ones — bases such as acceptance of experts' implicit ontological claim that the lay person or learner is not a competent judge of the validity question at issue and should accept the superior cognitive authority of the expert or teacher. The acceptance by children of the views of adults about almost anything, or the acceptance by women of the views of men about the things men are supposed to know that women don't, are also examples of this.

Utterances occur in social space and time as real events. We speak of utterances 'having' meaning, but it might be better to speak of hearers endowing them with meaning. As mentioned above, one aspect of this meaning is Perry's notion of the 'proposition created by an utterance'. Grice has a broader concept of such meaning. He talks of 'occasion' meaning[15] — the full meaning of uttering an utterance when and where and how it was uttered. Technically speaking, utterances may be distinguished from 'sentence tokens' (utterances give many tokens, including those of sentence types), 'sentence types' ('The cat sat' is the same type, spoken or in morse code) and 'propositions' (as the meanings of declarative sentence types). Utterance meaning must be distinguished from these more fragmentary analytically separable kinds of meaning. Utterance meaning involves multiple analytically separable dimensions of meaning, but these must be seen as occurring together, in a context, and in a mutually conditioning manner. That is, an utterance must be interpreted in a holistic way through an interpretive 'story' which takes account of and harmonises all the separate dimensions of meaning — existentially (in its assumptions about or references to the world, as in, for instance, its propositional content), interpersonally (in its being socially appropriate to express such assumptions about the world, given the interpersonal context), expressively (in providing an authentic expression of relevant feeling-states of the speaker). Of course, the utterance should also be intelligible at the level of its 'dictionary' or linguistic meanings.

Functional validity derives from a speaker's accomplishment in imbedding utterances simultaneously in relations with reality, other people and self. This capacity in a speaker is what is called communicative competence. We don't regard a speaker as competent if the grammatically correct utterances they can produce are socially unacceptable, like the apocryphal case of the person who learns a language from a sabotaged phrase book and asks a respectable lady a question like, 'Am I very sorry for your very pleasant bottom?' This competence rests on common ontological presuppositions. At the unexamined level these are part of the life-world. Many classrooms are characterised by communicative relationships which suppress differences in ontological presuppositions and assume asymmetrical characteristics for categories of participants. This often excludes the life-world resources of learners. Habermas analyses the kind of suppression that can occur phenomenologically.

How Our Ontological Assumptions Define Our Roles as Knowers

Habermas argues that while the ontological presuppositions of speakers may vary in content they involve common general structures of world relations. There are four basic 'worlds':[16]

1. a posited common objective world,
2. a social world with which one may relate in relating to that objective world,
3. an inner world of the self, and
4. the world of language.

Habermas' distinctive contribution is the argument that the set of possible relations between these worlds formally defines the *possible set* of recognisable (i.e.

meaningful) and therefore criticisable 'actions' (including validity claims) and of basic types of relationships between parties to communication. In short, the ontological presuppositions of members of the epistemic community *concerning themselves and others as interlocutors* in relation to the objective world, determine the range of forms of validity question about which they can effectively make judgements in a community of inquiry.

Habermas distinguishes among four basic kinds of action, each communicatively co-ordinated in a different way:[17]

1. Strategic action involves the '... interlacing of egocentric calculations of utility [where the degree of conflict and cooperation varies with the given interest positions]'.[18] A relatively pure example of this might be found in, say, negotiations between warring armies. In this form of action, actors are concerned with the choice of the most efficient means to given or egocentric ends.

2. Normatively regulated action occurs when members of a social group share common values and norms, instilled through socialisation, and where they can point to these norms as a justification for their actions.

3. Dramaturgical action occurs where groups represent a public or audience for others and actors manage the expression of their subjectivity in a process that has been called 'the presentation of self'.

4. Communicative action refers to the situation where actors seek to reach an understanding about their common situation and their action plans in order to reach an agreement which permits the co-ordination of action. A sub-type of this action is a 'pure' conversation where the goal is not the co-ordination of action but that of reaching an understanding in itself. This is called conversational action and is the action form associated with rational inquiry.

A typology of kinds of rational action and associated forms of critique may be constructed. The first three types appear in Table 1.[19]

Strategic action either succeeds or fails, and is thus criticisable, according to an appropriate (i.e. effective) or inappropriate choice of means to given ends. Normative action is judged as acceptable or unacceptable normatively because of a match or mismatch of action and norms. Dramaturgical action may fail if the performance given is regarded as insincere because actions in the outer world are not seen to conform to revelations about the inner world.[20]

In the fourth form of action the possibility of genuine (i.e. transcendental) rather than culturally encapsulated critique emerges for the first time, since utterances are relativised 'against the possibility that their validity will be contested by other actors'.[21] The definition of the situation is a specific segment of

TABLE 1 *Types of rational action and critique*

Type of action	Character	Starting point	Type of critique
1. Cognitive-instrumental (or strategic) actions	Conditions to be satisfied to reach ends specified	Specification of ends	Failure of ends/means matching
2. Normatively regulated actions	Normatively appropriate conduct	Identification of relevant norms	Critique of non-conformity
3. Expressive actions	Revealing inner feelings	Discovering what we feel	Critique of non-match of actions with feelings

the systematic common framework created by the intersection of worlds. A difference between actors can evoke a process of exploration of the world of the other:

> For both parties the interpretive task consists in incorporating the other's interpretation of the situation into one's own in such a way that in the revised version 'his' external world and 'my' external world can — against the background of 'our' lifeworld — be relativized in relation to 'the' world, and divergent situation definitions can be brought to coincide sufficiently. Naturally, this does not mean that interpretation must tend in every case to a stable and unambiguously differentiated assignment. Stability and absence of ambiguity are rather the exception in the communicative practice of everyday life. A more realistic picture is drawn by the ethnomethodologists — of a diffuse, fragile, continuously revised and only momentarily successful communication ...[22]

A form of communication in which interlocutors are prepared to re-examine their basic beliefs — their culture — is of obvious relevance for education in a time of unprecedented need for intercultural co-operation to ensure the species' survival on the planet. It may also be directly related to teaching situations where cultural or sub-cultural differences exist between teachers and learners. Clearly, the issue of gender may be examined from this standpoint. Not so obviously, this position is simply a restatement of the communication situation that should obtain wherever critical teaching and learning take place. The capacity to hold one's own beliefs open to question, in conjunction with a recognition of the different beliefs of another and the possibility that they may be valid, is a necessary, if not sufficient, condition for *social* problem solving in general and the cultural universalisation of problem solving in particular.

Dewey, Mead and Habermas

In order to draw out the educational significance of Habermas' view of the connection between meaning and validity it is necessary to develop an analysis of teaching/learning processes in school situations in action theoretic terms and to place communicative actions within this analysis.

Dewey developed an argument of this kind, using the ideas of George Herbert Mead. Since Dewey's views are likely to be more familiar to many readers than Habermas' it may be useful to try to put Habermas' ideas in the form of a reconstruction of Dewey's. Using Dewey also lets us take advantage of his account of problem solving, discussed earlier.

Dewey analyses interaction in terms of behaviourist interaction, but his approach differs from the stimulus–response behaviourism of a Skinner. Dewey is not a methodological individualist but speaks of systems of purposive behaviour of collectivities of individuals. He connects interaction closely with knowledge and knowledge closely with speech: 'The object of knowledge or speech is the consent of the co-ordinated response of speaker and hearer; the object of affirmation is the confirmation of co-adaptive behavior.'[23] This is a social and intentional model appropriate to the co-operative and co-adaptive problem-solving behaviour of intelligent organisms. Dewey's theory of the interpretation of meanings as something which occurs in 'immanent temporal wholes', which themselves occur in situations which may become 'objectively'[24] problematic or 'questionable', has much in common with the thrust of Habermas' analysis. Situations include the whole organism–environment totality, including the state of culture. When they become problematic it may be for many reasons, but when they do the human part of the process is involved because the needs of the persons involved are not being adequately met. If we are lucky, the problem may sometimes solve itself, through accidental environmental changes; unfortunately, many of the problems we seem to face today are going to require more deliberate and rational methods and more painful personal and cultural change.

Dewey's pedagogy consists primarily in teachers structuring classroom situations and providing resources so that this questionability and its associated needs might be dealt with by the students. However, Dewey's choice of examples, at least in most of what he wrote about education, tends to be confined to task-oriented or strategic behaviour involved in such pedagogy, although, for instance, he was open, in principle, to the analysis of the co-adaptive (or perhaps we should say, meta-adaptive) behaviour involved in examining and improving the value systems which define strategic goals in the first place, as his distinction between 'instrumental' and 'final' meanings and his discussions of value exploration and development indicates. The task-oriented behaviour he usually discussed was also associated with biological, cognitive and social needs of a relatively basic kind. He seldom discussed the possible presence in classrooms of the kind of needs he himself was presumably meeting by carrying out his own philosophical work, although he discussed this elsewhere.

Dewey's physicalism, too, tended to come through in his choice of exemplars, and thus, to an extent, his analysis, limiting it to the co-ordination of behaviour in orientation to solving physical problems and their associated schemata.[25] *Democracy and Education* concentrates on the construction by the teacher of a task environment, exemplified primarily by tasks with a physical system of reference, as epitomised by the science classroom experiment.

Despite these problems, Dewey's way of seeing the whole situation and context as problematic, rather than seeing the problem as defined by the subjective view of only one category of participant in the situation, has considerable advantages for us. By redefining problems we open up room to redefine what can count as solutions. We can now see problems and solutions 'ecologically' or holistically.

In his discussion of Mead,[26] Habermas moves in this direction. He shows that it is not enough to reject the individualistic paradigm of consciousness and avoid reductionist behaviourist accounts of meaning, although this is an important step. Linguistically mediated interaction involves several possible modes:

1.   the co-ordination of goal-directed behaviour,
2.   the teaching or socialisation of learners by bringing them *into* purposeful situations where action is co-ordinated by speech.

Both Mead and Dewey recognised this but Habermas adds something else which he places at the centre of his approach:

3.   the goal of achieving understanding itself.

While Dewey clearly recognises the necessity of cognitive consent (or in Habermas' terms: 'coming to an understanding') the details of this are not well developed in his discussion. Mead's analysis, on which he drew, completely failed to address this third mode of linguistically mediated interaction. When Dewey says 'Meanings do not come into being without language, and language implies two selves involved in a conjoint or shared undertaking'[27] he reaches

Habermas' fourth type of action, but not the sub-type of conversational action, which for Habermas is the centre of things. Thus, we may be tempted to add '... including the undertaking of simply sharing understanding itself'. Dewey recognised the importance of communities of inquiry, but the limitations of his analysis of communication meant that this recognition was not fully integrated into his work at all levels. Dewey's position is reminiscent of the transitional position Habermas adopted in *Communication and the Evolution of Society* (1979) immediately before his 'paradigm shift'. In that book he clearly identifies problems and their solutions with the organism–environment totality in a manner very close to Dewey's account:

> We may also speak of evolutionary learning processes on the part of societies, insofar as they solve system problems that present evolutionary challenges. These are problems that overload the adaptive capacity available within the limits of a given social formation ...[28]

He also speaks of individual developmental problems in the same holistic framework. In this transitional work, the process of communication and understanding was a problem-solving means to evolutionary achievements for both individuals and groups. Today, in a world where the biological dimension of our social life is coming into clearer focus, we might well view the evolutionary process as having a fully ecological and environmental dimension, too.

Only after the paradigm change did Habermas place the question of communication and understanding at the centre rather than the periphery of his model of inquiry. Dewey's model retains a reverse hierarchy, based on a hierarchy of needs. This implies that understanding yourself, others and the world is something you get around to only after your belly is full and you have put understanding to work first of all as a means of co-ordinating the food-acquiring activities of the group. Like Mead, Dewey relies on a reconstruction of the biological evolution of intelligence in which the means of satisfying basic needs are seen as evolving prior to those for satisfying higher needs. However, the sequence of development does not necessarily determine the sequence of use. Habermas' more Kantian analysis cuts the model of inquiry free of this connection. I think Habermas might well argue that it is when your belly is empty, maybe even at the point of death itself, that you most need to make sense of the world. I certainly do. Dewey did not share Mead's version of behaviourism, but he did not always escape from its pull.

Thus, there is a dimension of analysis prior to that which dominates *Democracy and Education* and *Experience and Nature*. In these, his central educational works, Dewey typically depicts the teacher and students standing side by side facing a task or problem situation. The virtue of this is that the teacher has at least moved from the rote-choir master's position at the front of the room.

The relationship of student to problem is brought into the foreground. But the picture is still incomplete. The teacher is standing *beside* the student but facing the task, not the student. If there is an emphasis, it is on the relationships between the two and the task, not upon the discourse, although a discourse is present in Dewey's picture.

Habermas' analysis creates a different picture. It focuses our attention more firmly on the student–task relation as an episode in an ongoing conversation between student and teacher about the nature of the world and the student's world-relations. This is an I–(It)–Thou relationship. It locates the student/teacher interaction much more firmly in a subject matter-oriented community (ideally a community of inquiry).[29]

We are now in a position to ask: What kind of action is a teaching action? Clearly, teaching can involve things like presentation of self to an audience ('good teachers have to be good actors'), and teaching/learning interaction takes place within a normative framework and may even involve discussion of whether or not classroom actions meet normative requirements or not, but neither dramaturgical nor normatively regulated action is central to the teaching process. They are, rather, means to create conditions under which teaching might take place, at least, insofar as one places the (rationally based) acquisition of knowledge and dispositions at the heart of one's definition of education. However, linguistically mediated interaction of the kind with which Dewey was mainly concerned — the consensual co-ordination of action plans (including plans for communicative action) — is also only a means to teaching/learning rather than a central feature of it. The problem-solving process *co-ordinated by* such interaction might bring us closer to the mark. There at last, in the formulation of theory and hypothesis by the child, the trying out of this theory, the experience of success and failure etc., we come upon something central to teaching/learning. But is this helping role, so often identified as the main pedagogical implication of Dewey's work, the only role for the teacher? Where would Socrates stand in such an account? As argued above, there is a third set of possible relations, a three-way process. Without rejecting the helper role component, let us locate it in teacher–student discourse about the world.

The link between the making of validity judgements and the act of interpretation permits us to get at a key psychological truth concerning learning, understanding and motivation, because this link is not simply cognitive but manifold. We do not simply agree or disagree with cognitive claims which arise randomly and either fit or do not fit some cognitive schema we have. We judge incoming content both cognitively and non-cognitively. This means that learners make judgements about the whole range of claims teachers make (including implicit claims) when the teachers are telling them some fact or theory. Among the claims that are made are: that what is said is in some sense 'relevant', that it connects up with the rest of the curriculum in some way, that what is being claimed at any point 'leads somewhere' and that it will all eventually 'make sense'. Students may not share the teacher's ideas about relevance as many teachers have discovered when they have been asked the dread question, 'Is this in the exams?'

These claims open up a range of possible learning/teaching role relationships and positionings, from a relationship where there is a great deal of patience required of learners, who often have to wait a long time to see connectedness or relevance and often do not see it at all, to a relationship where relevance for pupils is more or less guaranteed because of anchorage in the pupil's problematic but the priorities of the adult world may not be met.

A similar dimension exists in the area of expressive claims. Indications, for instance, of whether or not the speaker believes or strongly believes or doubts a theory or factual claim, or perhaps complacently assumes the complete truth of what is said, are always present in talk. Indications of the importance of a subject, love for a subject and the like also fall into this domain. These are claims about the relationships of persons to ideas and contexts and have obvious motivational and educational relevance.

The three dimensions of validity condition each other and are interpreted through a consistent story. Through such claims the learner, too, is given a certain room for manoeuvre, is made the subject of expectations. A teacher's love for a subject, his or her enthusiasm and sense of its importance are all claims on the learner's potential love for the subject. Through these opportunities and through the way learners take them up, learners become self-creating as knowers, and in turn, by their resistance and response, create teachers as teachers and thus as knowers too. The responsibility of teachers for the influence they inevitably exert over learners as knowers is greater than the kind of mutual influence and responsibility that may characterise members of a community of, say, scientific colleagues.

What happens when knowledge selected through another's problematic (possibly that of a remote committee of experts, or even the problematic of another time and place) is the basis of the present curriculum? What sort of relationship between teacher and learner is necessary for this knowledge not only to be accepted as cognitively valid but as important and worth knowing? Conversely, what sort of work of self-creation must a dutiful learner do in such circumstances? The invitation to step into another's shoes and try on their love of their subject for size might be a fine way for learners to open up to new possibilities, but, under slightly different circumstances, perhaps better described by 'demand' rather than invitation, learners may instinctively reject the imposition of what after all is a web of facts, relevances and feelings, never just a set of facts, and is therefore a part of a way of life.

Differences in class, gender, culture and biography may make the taking up of an educational invitation impossible, but they are even more likely to create resistance to 'instructional' demands. In turn, such refusal may well be taken as indicative of a lack of 'ability' or having a bad 'attitude' and is never without cost or risk in a system of unequal power to assess and label.

4 Discourse and Development

Distortions of Communication

So teaching action involves student/teacher discourse about the world. But this discourse need not be rational. It might not be 'discourse' in Habermas' ideal sense, but dialogue constrained by limitations, by teachers' authority, by taboos and no-go zones. The teacher might browbeat the pupil. We need some critical apparatus to allow us to judge between discourses, because the trappings of discourse can be used coercively.

In his analysis of distorted communication, Habermas identifies the strategic use of language as an ideological device, at least, the concealed strategic use of language. Using language act theory he shows how people can use language strategically *through* using it apparently communicatively. They make claims about truth, relationships and feelings, but the purposes of a series of claims to which the hearer is expected to respond as valid claims is to manipulate the hearer. Consider the example of the used car salesperson:

SP:	Hi, there! I'm Joe. You've come to the right place for a real deal, we're closing down and we're overdue to get rid of all our stock.
Customer:	Uh. Uh.
SP:	What sort of..What's your name ...
C:	Bob.
SP:	What sort of car you you looking for, Bob?
C:	A compact, maybe coupla years old.
SP:	Hey! Bob, your luck's in. We just had a terrific Chevvy traded the other day. Only one year old.
C:	I think that's maybe too expens ...
SP:	No way, Bob. Listen, Bob. We want to do the right thing by ya. We'll make the price right.

Here there are truth claims ('we're closing down': they've been 'closing down' for years), claims of an interpersonal kind (the use of first names: we are only here to help our friends) and no doubt all sorts of non-verbal indications of friendly sincerity. (Apologies to all honest used car salespersons.) The purpose of all these claims is to manipulate the customer into a situation where they feel *obliged* to buy the car. Perhaps all this manoeuvring is obvious enough to the experienced customer but the point is that the manipulative use of social conventions still exercises constraint on the responses of even experienced buyers. A boundary of impoliteness must be crossed, with perhaps a perceptible effort, if a customer were to answer the question 'What's your name?' with a surname after the salesperson had offered a first name: 'Hi there! I'm Joe ...'.

Now, the problem with this form of manipulation is not simply that the claims made are false, it is that the most important communicative intention — to sell, say, a *particular* car, whether you want it or not — might still be concealed. Maybe the car dealership has been stuck with a lemon, and then you've come along ...

Concealed intentions, in which those they are concealed from do not figure as ends in themselves, but as means to others' goals, are problem enough from a moral standpoint. But consider what happens when the dialogue is in the area of deciding on the truth or falsehood of knowledge claims, where the action or task is not about beliefs and the like as adjuncts to the pursuit of some other goal but the task of inquiry itself. What sort of strategic goals could exist in such a context? The aim of discovering the truth is not defined as a strategic goal in this context because the truth is mutual, and you may remember that 'strategic' is defined in the present argument as the pursuit of ego's goals irrespective of other people's. A strategic goal in this context could only be something like getting other inquirers to accept a version of knowlege that for some reason you want them to accept, irrespective of whether they rationally assent to it or not. It may be that you believe it to be true, or it may be that you want to spread a falsehood for other reasons (like government censors in wartime), but either way, the situation has a common strategic property, whatever its moral justification might be (you say 'sincerely' to the roundhead soldiers: 'The priest went thataway', when he is concealed in the priest's hole all along).

The issue is not that the teacher who acts this way has bad intentions. The teacher may act this way because of pressure of time, and with the intention of teaching truths it is in the learner's interest to know, and even with the belief that the learner would want to learn these things, if only they were mature enough to understand what they will need in later life, etc, etc. The issue is that when teachers act this way they deprive the learner of the opportunity to make a rational response to the knowledge claim concerned. Worse than that, they constrain the learner to make a response on the basis of a quite different kind of validity claim — that of the teacher's authority. Authority replaces reason as the basis of the pupil's response, sowing the seeds of perhaps lifelong habits of acquiescence to authority. When one aspect of our relationships overrides another, so that the forms of validity do not mutually support each other, we see a distortion of our rational capacity. When the truth of what is said is not allied to a relationship between the person who makes the truth claim and the hearer, which leaves the claim open to rational question, and the expressed feelings of the speaker are insincere or, in their own way, demanding of commitments beyond those which the consideration of argument and evidence by the hearer warrant, a distorted communicative situation is created. The learner is being treated as if he or she was less than human, or, at the least, a lesser human. But you may say that we are dealing with children's learning. Is there some sense in which children are somehow less than fully human (adults) and does this justify communication with them that is aimed at getting them to accept or believe something rather than getting them to make rational judgements about knowledge claims? To repeat something said earlier: Is our aim to create true belief or true believers?

An important qualification here is that the problem we are addressing is the ideological distortion of communication. There may be circumstances where individuals all act strategically and are aware that that is how they are acting. This occurs in many games. If a teacher and pupils agree to 'get through' a part of the curriculum, because they have fallen behind and it is 'in the exams', the interaction may be characterised by the 'interlacing of egocentric calculations of utility', but this need not be, in itself, a moral problem. The problem lies at a different level — at the level of the decisions about curriculum and examining practices — not the level of distorted communication in the classroom.

And there is a little more to it than that. The three general types of truth claim are found in each and every utterance. Each utterance has to function effectively in regard to its direct or indirect implications about the way things are, about the relationship between utterer and hearer, given the first set of claims, and with regard to indications given about the speaker's feelings about the first two sets of claims. The emotional and interpersonal dimensions are evoked even when the surface form of the utterance is 'statement talk'. When teachers pursue a concealed strategic intention, however benevolently they conceive of it, the distortion reaches into all the dimensions of language function. There is a tacit understanding that the pupil *will* accept the truth claims being advanced (i.e. will accept the claims of the language acts), and the relationship is no longer that of fellow inquirers, or even master to apprentice, as the structure of the talk shows. One party to the interaction, the teacher, is firmly in control of the agenda and line of questioning/presentation of material. There is no room for pupil questioning, doubting, or seeking more information. And the feeling dimension, which is close to the wellsprings of motivation, is subtly distorted, too. The teacher's communication of feelings, largely non-verbal, is not now concerned with the levels of confidence, or doubt, that one might have in various parts of the knowledge-story being presented. It is not now concerned with conveying a sense of awe at the elegance or beauty of the argument, or excitement, even vicariously, at reliving a moment of discovery. It is no longer concerned with any of those feelings that relate to our reasons, our need to reason, and our *delight* in reasoning. All these things become, at best, pale shadows of what they could be. Instead, the dominant feeling tone becomes rather like that which we are familiar with from arguments we once got into where the other person's goal was to convince us at any cost. There is also a concern that a line of argument be understood. But these are the shallower waters of human reasoning, not the deep intrinsic currents that move children to pleasure in learning.

The Ideal Speech Situation

The circumstances under which people in dialogue can treat each other (and reflexively themselves) as reasoning, feeling beings, without hindrance or constraint, have been called the Ideal Speech Situation.[1] One point to make about the ISS from the beginning — it does not and cannot exist. Rather it is a logical type. If you look at a communication situation and identify in it some constraint on the process of the participants freely weighing arguments and evidence, whether that constraint is from without (social) or from within (psychological), the very identification of these circumstances as *constraints* on the free examination of argument and evidence *implies* a hypothetically less constrained situation in which the inquiring community is better able to be rational. The use of any conceptual framework which implies the possible presence or absence of obstacles to the judgement of reasoning agents implies some comparative dimension of more or less constrained situations. From a conceptual point of view, once this dimension is in place, there is no obvious stopping place until you reach a hypothetical, indeed, counterfactual, end point — the idea of *un*constrained discourse. The factual situation stops where the historical or biographical situation stops, which is with the presently prevailing level and types of constraints. The ISS holds out the possibility of going further.

Although it has been misused as a utopian judgemental device to condemn all existing situations out of hand (because all have fallen short), its appropriate use is as a logical tool. We can try to identify existing constraints, even ones that seem quite justified to us, and imagine the situation with these removed. We can act, practically, to actually remove them, and see what results.

When we talk of a speech situation, we speak of speakers and their opportunities to speak, their speaking roles, if you like. Habermas' analysis of this used a conceptual framework drawn from a type of linguistic pragmatics. He used Wunderlich's set of grammatical and lexical devices for dialogue — the

dialogue constitutive universals.[2] These included categories of words or grammatical devices which identified self and other, things spoken about, time,
modality and the like. The ISS was defined in terms of symmetry of opportunity
to use the dialogic resources of language. Later[3] Habermas redefined part of this
analysis in terms of language act theory, as we have already seen in the previous
chapter. Later we will be restating this once again — in terms of systemic linguistics. The form of action which Habermas calls conversational action approximates the ideal speech situation. In this form of action, there is an intention of
openness, even if the present level of development of individuals or society does
not actually permit it.

This brings us to Habermas' second main point about the ISS. The ISS may
not actually exist, but in communicative action, particularly conversational
action, our behaviour proceeds, to an extent, *as if* it did exist. We assume the
possibility of openness. How is this possible? The form of action where we seek
to reach an understanding about what to do (communicative action) or about the
nature of things (conversational action) is action with an intention of understanding the other *and* reaching the truth, solving the problem and so on. Indeed,
as we have seen, understanding each utterance involves making validity judgements about its claims. Now, our good intentions may not be absolute. There
may be limits to how much that we hold sacred we will willingly allow to be
questioned, and so on. But we proceed under an intention of openness, of really
understanding. To the extent that we do this, we too assume the possibility of the
ISS. The idea of perfect understanding is inherent in the everyday idea of *really*
understanding someone. To enter into this kind of action, we put at least some of
our beliefs up for grabs. It is like starting to climb a mountain. We may not
entirely believe we will go all the way to the top, but we haven't decided in
advance just how far we will go. If we had, we couldn't, in one sense, be said to
be setting out to climb *the mountain*.

The ISS is not itself a measure of communicative distortion, but a tool to
assist in measuring it. We are dealing here with a particular set of moral
questions, those which arise from the act of communicating. This set of
questions is broad in scope, because, in a sense, all meaningful action
communicates, that is, is semiotic. When we utter a sign, even if that sign is to
wear certain clothes rather than others, we make, as the advertisers would have
it, 'a statement'. The questions concerned arise in the act of communicating:
questions of truthfulness, appropriate speaking, sincerity and the like. These are
to be distinguished from the intended courses of action in which they may be
involved. We may tell a lie in order to provoke a quarrel. The lie is merely a
means to another end, which may or may not be morally acceptable in some set
of circumstances. While the giants quarrel, Jack may escape. Alternatively, he
may steal one giant's gold to cast the blame on the other. This accomplishes the

same end by non-communicative means. Telling a lie may be justified by circumstances, but the circumstances do not make the lie go away. Any argument to justify the lie will be an argument, in part at least, about circumstances. When we begin to open up the issues in this argument, we rely on a discourse in which lies are no longer told, or we are unable to proceed. Discourse is a context in which the act of telling an untruth is intrinsically wrong because the circumstances are those of truth seeking. However, generally speaking, all actual, historical circumstances require other circumstances to be taken into account. In a way, we always need to lie, or better, we are unable to tell the whole truth. For this reason, the application of an ideal of perfectly transparent speaking as a moral measure of real situations, even those of inquiry, is utopian. What it can do is assist us in recognising those asymmetries and distortions that do exist. Judgements about the morality or otherwise of these ways of speaking is another matter. We will come to that in a moment.

Many concrete situations exist in which a degree of asymmetry of speech roles is entirely rational and appropriate. The division of labour in society (e.g. specialisation) means that the physician may ask more questions of the patient than the patient does of the physician, or at any rate, questions of a different kind. If one were to find a situation where the patient did not get a chance to ask any questions or even the questions they wanted to have answered, one might, given specific and concrete knowledge of the state of medical knowledge, the patient, the illness, and so on, be able to conclude that a given situation was asymmetrical in a way or in a degree which did manifest oppression. This conclusion could not be validly reached in the abstract, as it were, through the ideal of total symmetry or Foucault's implicit appeal to the notion that power is totally incompatible with truth.

Much the same might be said about the need, in large social formations, to co-ordinate the activities of large numbers of people. We may soon be forced by environmental disaster to achieve such co-ordination on a global scale. In such circumstances there may be a need for specific types and degrees of asymmetry. The issue is whether the asymmetry present in a given situation is functionally justified and whether some safeguarding apparatus or process (such as an electoral process) is present. Post-modernism's genealogical anthropology, properly used, can assist in the analysis and uncovering of this asymmetry, but not in its evaluation.

To trace the origins of a set of concepts, terms and ways of speaking (a 'discourse' in Foucault's sense) can help us to understand how the interests of some social arrangement of power can get built into a set of laws, theories, practices and ways of interacting with categories of people — ways of 'creating' them *as* the kind of people we define them as being. However, this anthropology of meanings cannot evaluate such discourses. The fact of asymmetry is not necessarily an evil. To show this we need to make a value judgement and that is the business of critique.

From time to time distortions of speech may occur in relationships which are generally symmetrical. Even good friends are not always sincere, truthful interlocutors. But the critical appraisal of distortions in communication is more concerned with structured distortions — distortions that reflect relatively permanent asymmetries in the relationships of socially recognised categories of people, asymmetries which prevent whole categories of people participating in defining their own lives and values. Appraisal of this kind is called 'ideology critique'. Here ideology is defined as a set of practices which construct reality from the perspective of the existential interests of one category of people rather than from a universal human perspective.[4] Ideologies, in the sense of sets of ideas and theories, may be a product of these practices, but are only sustained by practices that prevent discourses which might undermine them (and that promote discourses which support them). Ideology critique is concerned primarily with the effects of power, defined as the ability of one category of people to get another category of people to do what the first group want even if the second group don't want to. Authority is the situation which arises when the oppressed category (the ones who have to do what they don't want to do) comes to accept that those whom they serve have a right to tell them what to do. Sometimes authority is justified by circumstances, but its mere existence does not justify it. The aim of those in power, insofar as they want a peaceful life, is to turn their power into authority. One way of doing this is to promote a moral theory which justifies the situation, another is to make the state of affairs seem natural and unchangeable rather than a product of changeable practices and human definitions. Ideology critique thus concerns itself with concealed practices which create such meanings and the general dispositions to accept rather than inquire into them, and so distinguish between authority which is justified and that which is not. This conception of critique is one in which it is seen as a process which can transcend particular historical circumstances but not as a process which is simply and totally transcendent of all history. To transcend particular cicumstances is simply to evolve, to go forward, but there remain limits. You are still *in* history.

Thus, I can give an answer to a friend of mine who loves to play the devil's advocate. He asked me why I was so keen on education which taught students to inquire. I gave him three answers. The first concerned economic growth and the flexible creative workers needed in our economy. But that wasn't good enough. The second was the need to solve global political and environmental problems for the survival of the species. His reply to this was that all that was required was that a few leaders get together and agree to oppress everyone else, within 'the limits of sustainable growth', of course. The third was a moral one. I said that I didn't want to be forced to live my one and only life in a reality created entirely by others *for* others, that I wanted to create, too. And that I believed that the only way I could achieve this was if enough other people felt the same way. Otherwise powerful people would own my life — I would owe my soul to the company store, as a 1950s song had it. The fact that I could already be creative of my own life to some extent was due to a lot of people fighting for just this sort of right in the past, and their at least patchy success in creating the freedom for others to 'pursue happiness' in political liberty. And, what is more, I argued, what I am after will let us achieve the other goals as well, and far more efficiently than through systems of control and oppression. But can these goals be reached with children?

Education from Infancy

Strategic structures of communication in teaching are inherently indoctrinatory because the hearer is unable to take a rational position on validity claims which are concealed. But some would argue that such indoctrination is not necessarily incapable of being justified in the overall process of education of the young, provided views acquired in this way might eventually be rationally explored. In fact, some have argued that it is not necessary for pupils to have the opportunity for inquiry in order to be able to inquire later, and even that pupils below the age of adolescence are incapable of inquiry, and that attempts to encourage them to inquire are positively harmful. German liberal conservatives, such as Spaemann,[5] writing specifically against German critical theory of education, have argued that learners must first master bodies of knowledge before they can criticise them.

The traditional, common-sense idea of teaching seems to involve something very like this. As Oelkers[6] has argued, the traditional conception of the teacher is as a person entrusted with the task of pursuing the interests of the child on the child's behalf. But the liberal conception of education, since the Enlightenment at least, has held that the (at least eventual) goal of schooling is a state in which the teacher puts himself or herself out of business — the child reaches the stage of being able to think 'for herself'. Put together, the two views form a composite view which might be described as liberal conservative (the preferred label of many neo-conservatives). But, as Oliver[7] has argued, the problem for such views is the development of an adequate account of the process whereby teaching moves from one state to another: in terms of the present argument, from strategic communication structures,[8] which actually characterise most contemporary classrooms, to conversational ones. Spaemann, like most liberal conservative educators, has no account of the transition to critique. We may even suspect that he would not be particularly concerned if it did not occur.

Like Spaemann, J. S. Mill also argued that it was legitimate for adults to abridge the liberty of children because they were '… not capable of free and equal discussion'.[9] Other philosophers, such as Peters (and Dearden) have argued along similar lines '… the brute facts of child development reveal that at the most formative years of a child's development he is incapable of [a rational] form of life …'[10] In another place, Peters rejects progressive schools: 'Progressive schools therefore, which insist *from the start* in children making their own decisions and running their own affairs ignore the crucial role which the stage of conventional morality plays in moral development.'[11] Peters fears that if children are encouraged to criticise moral principles while still at this conventional stage,[12] i.e. at elementary school age, they will suffer from a loss of 'ontological security'.

However, Dewey suggested that the development of children's capacity to enter into discourse may not be like that: 'Any power, whether of child or adult, is indulged when it is taken on its given and present level in consciousness. Its genuine meaning is in the propulsion it affords toward a higher level.'[13] If so, teaching may be more like psychoanalysis. The capacity for children to enter into inquiry may develop gradually. In the process of analysis, analysts must adapt their communication to the appropriate stage of the analysis, changing their communicative role and their level and kind of communicative participation as their patients undergo or pass through stages of analysis such as transference. Specific stages of the process of analysis 'enable' specific kinds of communicative relationship.

We must turn to empirical studies of the development of children's capacity to enter into argumentation to understand the nature of this progression. The social-cognitive development of children may be described, at least for heuristic purposes, in terms of levels. Habermas and his co-workers adopted Kohlberg's model of moral development, with adaptations. In this model, at the first level children cannot be responded to as subjects who can be '… held responsible for actions with a view to generalised behavioural expectations'. At the second level the child associates norms of roles of family members and others, and group norms. Conventional responsibility emerges. Finally, at the third level actors can '… assert their identities independent of concrete roles and particular systems of norms'.[14] They become capable of a critique of norms on the basis of principles. As we move through the levels, actors' symbolic capacity becomes less context-dependent, more reflexive, abstract, individually differentiated and generalised.

Since inquiry is a social-relational accomplishment, the development of inquiry follows the social-cognitive developmental pattern, so Habermas and his co-workers widened Kohlberg's model to include the development of a capacity to enter into argumentation. Unlike the development of a capacity for moral judgement, the development of a capacity for argumentation, as conceptualised by Miller, one of Habermas' co-workers, incorporates the social capacity for *entering into* argumentation, as well as the mere cognitive capacity to generate or criticise arguments in some formal sense, as children might do when confronted by an experimenter describing argument scripts.

Miller, following a generally Piagetian methodology, but working with groups of children, has theorised a stage-like developmental process in respect of a capacity to enter into moral argumentation at various moral argument levels.[15] In the observation of group problem-solving argument among children discussed earlier (Chapter 2), Miller identifies the stages of argumentation in terms of the kind of problems which children can collectively solve in resolving a moral dilemma situation. At the first level, among children aged five years, the problem of the basis of justification is recognised and solved (what moral principles do you use?). At succeeding levels, problems of coherence (are we using the same principles?), circularity (are we going round in circles?), and language (are we using the same terms in the same way?) arise. All four levels are identifiable in the argumentation of older children, with, typically, a recapitulation of the developmental sequence in a series of contextual switches during the process of argument.

Miller argues that recognition of these problems and a capacity to solve them '... ontogenetically develop in a ... sequence'.[16] He argues that the first stage, of justification, manifests itself as early as two years, and he presents evidence, albeit somewhat sketchy, that the remaining 'stages' manifest themselves successively as children grow and develop.

If Miller is right, even in a most approximate way (and that is a question for further research), it suggests that children do have a capacity to engage in moral argumentation from an early age, certainly pre-school age, but that the nature of the problems of moral argumentation that they are able to resolve form a developmental sequence. Provided there are appropriate constraints on the problem situation, a three-year-old child can argue just as validly about a problem of justification (i.e. the relationships between an action and a norm) as you or I. Indeed, Miller's argument details the logical structure of such arguments in such a way as to show that there is no formal logical difference between a rational adult and the three-year-old child in this respect.

The approach adopted here bears a strong resemblance to Dewey's problem-solving method of pedagogy:

From the side of the studies [the disciplines of knowledge, R. Y.], it is a question of interpreting them as outgrowths of forces operating in the child's life, and of discovering the steps that intervene between the child's present experience and their richer maturity.

and

... the problem ... is just to get rid of the prejudicial notion that there is some kind of gap in kind (as distinct from degree) between the child's experience and the various forms of subject matter that make up the course of study.[17]

But what about the argument that, whatever children are capable of, it is unnecessary (and a waste of time) to bother with inquiry learning, because it is still possible to develop (the desirable) rational autonomy even though it is not exercised? This seems to be Peters' position.

While Peters tries to avoid specific pedagogical and curricular recommendations, it appears from his work that the methods available for the development (without exercise) of rational autonomy are rather limited. They must consist in some practices which are initiated and motivated by the teacher, such as the setting of exercises in skills or content knowledge deemed a part or a necessary but not sufficient condition of autonomy, training in the recognition of logically valid arguments, the learning of past critiques or the modelling of critique by the teacher. The teacher tells the students an argument, or reads out an account of the reasoning of, say, a great scientist, or sets exercises in logical analysis of arguments, demonstrates a law by conducting a demonstration experiment and so on. The student picks up the skills of logic, of structuring argument, recognises reasons given by teachers for accepting or rejecting evidence and so on. In short, the practice of skills in set exercises and experience of the arguments held valid by others is supposed to create rational development which can then manifest itself in the actual exercise of rational participation in argumentation when the circumstances are appropriate.

However, such an account would be one-sidedly cognitive. It ignores the interpersonal reality of argumentation, and the element of risk and engagement. From the standpoint of Habermas' approach to meaning and validity, it is an account which is simultaneously monological and narrow. It is monological because it fails to recognise that the resolution of validity claims is ultimately a social (i.e. dialogical) rather than an individual process and that validity only emerges in social engagement, engagement which, in turn, is only made possible by appropriate normative and emotional conditions. One gets the impression that many who learn about argumentation in the way suggested above would never dare to argue. The account is narrow because it fails to recognise that each and every utterance, even in the most abstract arguments, is multi-functional.[18] Interpersonal relationships and personal feelings are always communicated at the same time as statements about the world, even in primarily constative speech. It is in the normative and expressive relations of speaker and hearer that many of the social arrangements that block the exploration of validity questions in a rationally open way are located.

Much dialogue can take place within accepted norms, and under some expressive constraints, and cognitive progress of a limited kind might still be made. But sometimes cognitive dissonance, normative disagreement (e.g. about speaker roles) and the like emerge, and the dialogue may shift to a meta-level where the assumptions and procedures underlying the previous level of dialogue may themselves be directly discussed. Such shifts of level are normal parts of the process of argumentation as Miller's analysis also shows, and a necessary part of the expression of rational autonomy (conceived of as rational participation). Given that all actual dialogues take place in social and historical conditions of constraint, the capacity to make such shifts becomes crucial to the possibility of cognitive progress. The modelling of argumentative processes by teachers in a monological and narrowly cognitivist way is no preparation for the real hurly-burly of argument.

A capacity for recognising logical contradictions, conceptual confusions, statements unsupported by evidence and so on, however valuable, does not add up to a capacity for intellectual autonomy. Whatever the problems with 'capacity' as a concept, it is clear that the idea of a capacity for autonomy is vacuous unless it is a capacity for its exercise in the form of participation in forming validity judgements in actual social situations of unequal power and authority. Here, Habermas' distinction between linguistic competence and communicative competence is important. The former may be fully engaged in silent recognition but the latter only in participation.

If the possibility for rational response is realised only in open communication structures and if the capacity of the child for such responses exists from an early age, it is possible to link Dewey's emphasis on a careful structuring of the problem situations encountered in the educational environment with an emphasis on a parallel ordering of communication structures.

In the discussion of the developmental nature of children, we have again raised ontological questions and we have been able to point to some of the ontological assumptions about learners that might underlie perlocutionary conduct by teachers. The connection between meaning and meaningful communication and the possibility of learners exploring questions of validity has been deepened. But there is also an intimate connection between situations where learners are prevented from making rational responses to validity questions, for whatever reason, and failure by learners to *understand* or be able to *use* what the teacher intends to transmit. There are three possible responses to the validity claims which are part of the meaning of situated utterances — acceptance, rejection, or suspension of decision in the absence of sufficient information. The last form of response ought to be common if the claims being advanced are new to the learner. Opportunity to gather more information is implied in a situation where learning is the goal — learning, in the sense of rational learning which means learning based on rational responses to argument and evidence. But many classrooms are not characterised by the kind of teacher/learner relationship where suspension of judgement or the gathering of more evidence is encouraged. Where this is prevented, the learner can only acquire a schemata-disconnected kind of knowledge which is highly context-specific. I would want here to connect up with recent debate concerning the radically contextual character of much classroom learning and to point to a reason why most classrooms are 'decontextualised' in ways other than those suggested by their mere separation from the things learned about (e.g. a geography lesson about Peru being conducted in a classroom in New York).[19] Classrooms are decontextualised from the learner's point of view when the learners' feelings, their beliefs about what is important, their reasoning and their experience are not part of the assumed context of the teacher's communication.

Dewey recognised these problems quite clearly:

... one of the weightiest problems with which the philosophy of education has to cope, is the method of keeping a proper balance between the ... incidental and the intentional in education. When acquiring of information and technical intellectual skill do not influence the formation of a social disposition, ordinary vital experience fails to gain in meaning ... To avoid a split between what men consciously know because they are aware of having learned it by a specific job of learning, and what they unconsciously know because they have absorbed it in the formation of their characters by intercourse with others, becomes an increasingly delicate task with every development of ... schooling.[20]

There is also the germ of an argument here for the self-directed exploratory freedom Dewey enjoined. If the internal connection between meaning and validity places a great strain on the child's capacity to defer judgement when the incoming information is constantly novel, it is often the case that this strain leads eventually to a situation in which the kind of validity claims being made are not recognised at all. Unintelligibility can be produced by the failure of tacit validity claims to connect up with the child's ontology as well as by a simple failure of transmission of dictionary or surface meanings. The failure to connect with the child's schemata may be called 'framework failure'. When learning emerges from the *child's* problematic, this form of failure is far less likely.

I have argued that it is possible for children to argue just as validly as adults, within constrained problem situations. Further, if children do not engage in critique as they learn, they may not have the courage for critique later. Thus it is neither necessary nor desirable to wait until bodies of knowledge have been mastered (for Spaemann this seems to mean until one has taken a university degree) before engaging in critique. I also want to argue that it might not be *possible* to understand, let alone master, a body of knowledge unless there is engagement in critique.

In the complex set of possible forms of meaningful behaviour (action) which is available to the contemporary teacher, it is difficult to see what must be done and what avoided. But whatever values may motivate the teacher in this task, I cannot see that adopting an obscurantist position concerning the child's capabilities in linguistically mediated teaching/learning can improve matters. Just as interpretive observers who limit the postulated ontology of their subjects by ascribing more limited action forms to participants than they assume for themselves, may fall into the error of diminishing their subjects' human capacity, making them out to be the typical dumb savages of so much ethnocentric anthropology, or the dumb, benighted 'folk' of so much superior sociological analysis of everyday life, so too, the teacher can so easily settle for an ontology of the learner in which the full creativity of the learner's capacity for rational exploration and communication never becomes a resource for learning. As experienced classroom teachers know, the rejected creativity of the learner can nonetheless find its fulfilment in rejection of the teacher.

5 Towards a Critical Linguistics

From Language Acts to Language in Action

The time has come to move from the level of general theory to analysis of concrete speech. This is a move from the level of critical theory to actual critique. Critical theory reconstructs the general competencies of actors at a high level of abstraction, and does not take specific circumstances into account. It considers the general effect of kinds of circumstances but not of particular sets of circumstances. It is called reconstructive because it seeks to reconstruct the set of rules or the knowledge actual participants must have possessed in order to have done what they have been observed to do. In the same way as ethnolinguists documenting a new language, it is possible to do this from a few instances, and a representative sample is not always necessary. Critical theory can reconstruct in an armchair sort of way, but actual critique is safest when made by participants in real situations. There are two reasons for this. First, because the very making of such immanent critique *in* the situations where the practices of speaking tend to make persons into things, or represent their choices as if they were already fixed facts of nature, robs these practices of their ideological power. When outsiders do this it is less likely to be effective than when carried out by those whose interests are directly involved. Second, critique is best made inside situations because only insiders can really understand their own interests. True, we all can fail at this, but generally speaking, outsiders, however benevolent, cannot understand our own 'case' as well as we can.

The very *basis* of critique of practices, the ISS, plus a sense of beauty, moderation and balance, is available for critique precisely because participants themselves possess these things. Criticism arises within the social life that is its object. Situations and structures never exist in quite the way any one group of participants sees them, and social or cultural meanings are inherently and *essentially* ambiguous, even if some counter-meanings are almost subliminal. This is because meanings are a social construct, as well as an individual one, and represent the sedimentation of a history of compromise and accommodation between groups, as well as, in any particular and concrete manifestation of meaning, the biography of an individual who has lived within such social influences. We, as individuals, make meanings 'in our heads', but we are also beings whose meanings came to us in infancy and childhood through the filter of our parents, siblings and other persons. Meanings must always be held in tension between the whole society or language community and the local level, between these and the individual. The systematic critique of structures of classroom communication, in these terms, has barely begun. What you will find in the following chapters is only an illustration — a vicarious extension of reconstructive critique. It is a finger, but not the thing pointed at.

But even that pointing requires some conceptual development. An adequate descriptive linguistics is necessary to talk about situated language in any detail. The tool Habermas chose for an abstract, universal pragmatics, language act theory, is not adequate for this.

Habermas' language act analysis is intended to provide a universal formal pragmatics which is inherently critical and which provides the framework for any possible empirical pragmatics. He recognised the heavy burden of proof which such universal claims must bear.[1] Moreover, he argues, we cannot simply deduce from any general set of assumptions about language an account of the '... pretheoretical knowledge that competent speakers bring to bear when they employ sentences in actions oriented to reaching understanding'.[2] We can only try to reconstruct our intuitions about language. Any model we produce must be subject to the test of its empirical usefulness in explaining meaning systems or discourses and their development, patterns of communication, including distorted communication, and the linguistic development of individual capabilities for social action. The success of this form of analysis in any field must be attested in the same way as it would be when applied to the progress of science itself:

> it can hold up in the end only if reconstructive theory proves itself capable of distilling internal aspects of the history of science and systematically explaining, in conjunction with empirical analysis, the actual, narratively documented history of science in the context of its social development.[3]

Much the same might be said about the history of education. On the basis of his general theory of language, Habermas constructed a critical theory of mutual exploration of the validity claims inherent in all utterances and of the (counter-factual) conditions under which such exploration could take place. He also pointed to the general need for ego maturity if communicators are to be able to engage in critique of their own or their culture's view of the world, and in the necessary problematisation of parts of the life-world that critique involves. But Habermas reserved the term 'discourse' for the kind of communicative exploration that emerges when taken-for-granted aspects of the life-world are made theoretic and are subjected to disinterested appraisal. In most social situations, validity claims are made and resolved within the horizon of the taken-for-granted as speakers' claims are recognised as conforming to the background knowledge and institutionalised norms of the culture, and discourse, in Habermas' special sense, does not emerge.

In a close parallel with Halliday's set of existential/logical, interpersonal and textual functions, Habermas has argued that three kinds of rationally adjudicable validity claims are unavoidably raised in all speech. These four claims are:

1. that what is said is true;
2. that the saying of it is right or appropriate;
3. that the speaker is sincere or truthful; and
(4. that what is said is intelligible, well-formed, apt, etc.).

However, while Habermas sketches the steps whereby his formal or universal pragmatics might be employed to guide empirical pragmatics — by reintroducing actual contexts, sequences of speech acts, background worlds of participants and the like — he does not undertake this task himself and it is in precisely this area of application that the speech act theory he employs is weakest. The formal, distinct, complete, literally-meaning speech acts of Habermas' analysis lend themselves poorly to the real world of non-standard forms, oblique and elliptical meanings, irony, poetry, textual meanings, overlapping meanings, extra-verbally supplemented meanings etc. that he lists in his discussion of the problem.[4]

Moreover, the problem of developing an empirically satisfactory and consistent typology of language acts has not been solved. Ballmer and Brennenschul's[5] close analysis of Searle's fivefold language act classification, which Habermas uses, indicates that there are many problems. For instance, the notion that declaratives constitute a separate class is problematic since all classes of language act can be stated in a declarative manner. The distinction between directives and commissives is superficial, since they differ only in the addressee. Only expressives, representatives and directives remain, the three basic aspects of all signs (and incidentally, the three basic areas of validity claim identified by Habermas).

Language act theorists define particular language acts, somewhat circularly, by the use of certain verbs — expressives by the verb 'to express', for instance — but acts are functional categories and lexical markers are incidental to them. The same verbs can appear in utterances that clearly don't function expressively and other verbs appear in clearly expressive utterances. Distinctions between performatory and non-performatory verbs break down. In addition, the notion of illocutionary force is dependent on the separation of propositional force from the illocutionary, but there is no clear-cut way of doing this in every instance. While language act analysis may sensitise us to the possibilities of 'doing things with words' or even to the illocutionary dimension in all utterances, it is a tool which does not fare well in all the complexity of actual language *in situ*. Wunderlich provides a similar critique.[6]

In addition to problems of classification, there are problems in the theory of meaning, and in particular with the role of reference, associated with problems of specification of the propositional component.

A third, and in my view decisive, cluster of problems for a speech act theory of natural language may be found in the notion that speech acts are in some sense 'elementary units' of semantic analysis. This is also related to the problem of meaning. The identification of elementary units at the act level is a by-product of an earlier identification of sentences (and imbedded propositions) as elementary units of the expression of meaning (no doubt, in its turn a product of logical atomism!). But there are many difficulties for a theory of meaning which operates at the sentence level (or lower). Many of these are revealed when the object of analysis is a naturally occurring text, in a real context, rather than the impoverished contexts and atomised texts of the pages of philosophy books. Empirical linguistics, coping with naturally occurring texts, has been unable to make do with a theory of meaning that does not operate at a number of levels, including the supra-sentential. Meaning resides as much in texts, or even 'discourses' (in the recent French sense) as it does in utterances or acts. It resides in structures of metaphor, forward and backward relations *within* the text itself as it unfolds, and in situational and contextual relations as much as in language acts — or, to put it another way, it resides in action rather than acts.

To date, I am unaware of any satisfactory extension of speech act theory to the analysis of actual, situated texts.[7] I do not wish to argue that such an extension is not possible, but rather to suggest that there may be a way of avoiding the great labour that would be necessary in its development. I wish to contend that there already exists an appropriate form of analysis of situated speech methodologically rich enough to take on the complexities of speech-in-context. The relatively simple task (now that it has already been mapped for us) is to show that this form of analysis can be employed at the level of critical formal pragmatics.

The candidate for this task is systemic linguistics as developed by Halliday, Hasan and others. Systemic linguistics provides a general or universal level of analysis of language functions, through the concepts of field, tenor and mode and related existential, interpersonal and textual functions. But through the concepts of context of situation, context of culture, contextual configuration, genre and generic structure potential it provides a basis for the analysis of situated speech, particularly relatively orderly or institutionalised speech.

Halliday's conception of function is not a 'use' theory of function but what might reasonably be seen as an 'action' theory of function — it relates to the accomplishment of socially recognised tasks. Systemics also recognises the simultaneity and interrelatedness of all functions in each and every utterance, and the types of functions identified parallel those phenomenologically identifiable validity concerns which Habermas wishes to explore.

In addition, systemics provides an apparatus for the analysis of institutionally bound speech which is appropriate for dealing with whole structures rather than single utterances and for explicating the existence of particular forms or genres of speech and the generic speech role attitudes of participants, including the phenomenologies of participation which particular socially recognised classes of participants might possess. The analysis is also open to extensions into extra-verbal forms of communication. The questions that remain are:

1. Does systemics permit incorporation of a model for critique?
2. Does it permit a parallel account of the types of validity claims Habermas identifies?
3. Can a similar model of communicative distortion be constructed in systemics, that is, can we spell out the communicative consequences of contradictions in the conception of 'the task' in social situations?
4. Can institutionalised structures of distorted communication be identified using the concepts of systemics?

Although the Halliday/Hasan analysis does not overtly incorporate any notion equivalent to an ideal speech situation, the assumption in it of a common task definition and common norms actually tends to support Habermas' contention that speakers normally assume that the various validity claims of speech are validly made. It is relatively easy to restate Habermas' position in terms of systemics.

However, the systemic conception of context evolved towards a more critical position only in recent years, although one might argue that it was always implicit in it. As stated above, context of situation is analysed in terms of field, tenor and mode. Field is the existential dimension of situation, including the purpose or task, tenor that of social relationships (and presumably expression of feeling is part of that), and mode is the way the resources of language are drawn on by the actors in carrying out the task. In earlier applications of systemics there was no explicit reflexivity in the way these concepts were presented. Any reflexivity was provided by *the linguist's* own, non-linguistic theoretical resources, such as the application of the theory of social class. It came from outside, not from within the theoretical apparatus of systemics. Later developments in the concept of 'context', made in response to criticisms by Sbisa and Fabbri, and by Cicourel,[8] made the critical possibilities clearer, making the affinity between systemics and critical theory more visible.

In reply to the criticisms of these writers, Hasan[9] argued that to describe context in terms of social norms: '... is not to side with the group wielding power any more than to describe working class dialects is to bring about a social revolution ... The recognition of norms would be misleading if ... a scholar chose to ignore the presence of conflicting norms.' She recognises that contexts themselves are not fixed but negotiated and therefore available for change and contestation. Roles can be played with more or less individual role distance, and roles can change, but the individual actor is always faced with a *socially* given set of resources with which to begin to realise new possibilities.

However, Habermas' meta-pragmatics provides a possible systematic framework for the inclusion of these insights within the theory of meaning and language action which marries up nicely with the systemic empirical pragmatics. The theory would run this way: The assumption of the ISS by speakers is part of the context of all speech situations. All speakers are potentially aware not only of the gap between ideal and real but of the contrast between one speech situation and others. Contestation and critique are at least subliminally present in all historically occurring speech situations *as a part of the nature of speech communication itself.* All competent speakers are aware of differences in speech situations and can talk about these in commonsensical terms. They are also constantly making judgements about the rightness or wrongness of situations (often by default, it is true).

With Martin,[10] but for somewhat different reasons, I would argue that genres, roughly sets of structured expectations about speaking roles and how speech should proceed in given situations, are a form of *control by structure.* It is at the level of structure that we see the primary expression of ideology because it is at this level that speakers and categories of speakers (women, children, subordinates) come under the pressure of *structural expectation* to speak and therefore socially *be* in certain ways. However, I would also argue that not all structural expectations are ideological, since not all genres constrain the speech of socially recognised categories of speakers in oppressive rather than complementary forms of asymmetry.

To bring the analysis back to education, and to point to some of the critical resources that children might deploy in schooling talk situations, we can remember that, as Hasan tells us, children come to the different communicative environment of the school from their experiences in the family and peer group. They may also bring resources to bear from the culture. The experience of informal, relaxed and relatively open speaking in the family and peer group contrasts with the formality of the classroom. Children may not explicitly ask what justifies the formality, asymmetry and coldness of classroom talk, they may simply turn away from it to seek the warmth of the peer group and seek to bring that situation, unofficially, into the classroom — which, of course they do, and it is a very effective form of action-critique! The culture, too, may contain ideas about reasonableness and open speech which older children may draw upon to challenge some of the constraints the classroom typically places upon them. Children are aware, albeit not at the theoretic level, of when they are being treated as persons in an educational relationship and when as mere instructional objects.

The difference between 'educational' and 'instructional' here signals a difference between a normative or valuing process and a supposedly descriptive or value-neutral one. In using the term 'educational' this way, I am trading on the tendency among philosophers of education to adopt a normative definition for the term 'education'.[11] The contrast I seek to make is similar to that which is sometimes made between 'education' and 'training'. As a matter of fact, I do not believe that it is ever possible to carry out mere 'instruction'. The belief that this is possible I see as a mistake. When 'instruction' or 'training' is attempted I would want to define what is happening in terms of an attempt to close off and prevent certain kinds of learning while fostering others. Instruction is characterised by the kinds of not-learning it seeks to impose. Those who try to do 'instruction' are often engaged in the transmission of ideology; those who believe that they are merely instructing are themselves victims of ideology.

But to say this is not the same thing as saying that there should be no instruction in schools. We must be open to the possibility that instruction, involving the closing off of certain kinds of learning opportunities while pursuing others, may be justifiable in particular cases. However, if the view of instruction presented here is accepted, it is not possible to evaluate such instruction purely in terms of its efficiency and effectiveness as these are usually defined, that is, in terms of the economy of effort and degree of success which is associated with achieving the kinds of pre-decided learning being pursued. It is necessary to take into account the implications of the not-learning process, of the closing off of learning opportunities that may lead to new forms of problem solving.

Traditional forms of linguistic analysis of communication in school situations have not displayed a great deal of concern with critique of educational practices in this broader sense. Often the instructional objectives of the teacher (syllabus, textbook) have been taken for granted and criticism, if you can call it that, is confined to the appraisal of alternative communicative strategies for achieving them. In the nature of most research studies of classrooms there is no effective way for the researcher to show a concern for the long-term consequences of strategies that may promise, or even achieve, short-term success. The

degree to which immediately 'successful' instructional strategies may be responsible for the longer-term growth among pupils of either resistance or apathy is
not explored.

However, descriptive linguistics may be used critically. This occurs when
you have critical *linguists* (but not necessarily a critical *linguistics*). A critical
linguistics concerns itself directly with these longer-term questions since it sees
them as a part of language itself.

The focus of critical perspectives is upon improvement of human problem
solving. The immediate response of many to statements of the kind I have just
made is to protest that they, too, are concerned with the improvement of human
problem solving (possibly through trying to make instruction more efficient).
This may well be true, but the difference between critical and 'traditional' perspectives, as I wish to use the terms, does not lie in differences of motivation or
intentions among researchers using different 'paradigms'. It lies in whether or
not the paradigm used provides *within itself* a methodology for improvements to
be identified and made, or whether it merely permits the researcher to apply
some separate, essentially arbitrary normative framework (e.g. personal values).
Critical communication theory claims to be able to address the normative question within the framework of a single methodology, but the most common forms
of linguistic analysis applied to schooling do not.

Systemic linguistics provides a good starting point for the development of
a critical educational linguistics. Systemics is characterised by the anthropological insight that language normally means and functions against the background
of a culture, in which the communication situation itself and the roles of actors
in it are defined. Where the situations and roles are familiar and repeated, regular communication expectations are built up, and predictable linguistic structures
emerge. And, of course, as educators we are concerned precisely with communication rather than language as such, since the role of teacher, whatever else it
may entail, must involve some process of facilitating communication of ideas
(facts, stories, concepts etc.) from some persons to others.

Systemic analysis has the additional virtue that it is, as it were, open at the
sociological end. The way categories of people are assigned to roles, the way situations and situation types grow up in a society, the relation between one situation and another and the problems which arise in situations, can all be explored
in and through analysis of particular forms of situated communicative problem
solving.

It is this quality of systemic linguistics that Kress puts to work in his discussion of the role of power and ideology in communicative processes,[12] or, to
put it another way, his discussion of the way power is created and maintained

through particular communication structures. Essentially Kress argues that the sets of utterances (including non-verbal signs) produced in social interaction, which we will here call 'texts', are products of a social process whereby participants are 'constantly engaged in [language's] reconstitution and change'.[13] They do this because they are engaged in the reconstitution and change of the way society (i.e. other people) have defined them and the way other people consequently relate to them. Social life is very much concerned with relative prestige and reward. Even the most egalitarian societies are highly competitive. When a group of children vie with one another to see who will play the role of cowboy and who the destined-to-be-defeated Indian they are playing out a process which their parents, indeed the whole society, have already played out on a larger scale. And just as the Indians get tired of falling down dead and want to make a killing for a change, so the order of things in the wider society is subject to challenge. Hasan and Kress have both shown us many ways in which particular sets of roles manifest/create a 'discourse' (roughly a set of structures and a register) which in turn maintains and realises them. Social institutions such as buying and selling, marriage and the family, the workplace, the school, consist of clusters of norms/rules which define role relationships between categories of individuals, such as teachers/pupils or husbands/wives. These norms encompass mutual expectations concerning rights and obligations, but they also encompass communicative expectations — the sort of things particular categories of people are expected to say at particular times in particular situations. Much as the dialogue in a game of cowboys and Indians, as well as the action, has been culturally scripted according to a stereotyped and ideological view of American history, so the dialogue and action in all the dramas of life has already been (loosely) scripted. But social life operates under a double structure. Just as life defines roles, roles constitute and reconstitute life.

Accordingly, just as some of the actors in the children's game may become dissatisfied with their lot, actors in the game of life may strive to redefine situations and roles. Under such circumstances old scripts come under some strain. Things do not go according to expectations — the Indians start winning. What changes would a collection of husband/wife scripts stretching from, say, 1930 to 1990 reveal?

Kress identifies many features of language that reflect differences in 'power and prestige'. Some are structural and concern opportunities for particular categories of actors to speak, or to speak in a certain way, others concern the words used, others the theories of people's identities and motivations buried in particular metaphors, and others the way in which you can hide the true authorship or agency of a deed by grammatical choices such as the use of the passive voice by bureaucrats.

But the analysis tends to retain a certain dualism: 'An explanation for differing modes and forms of speaking can only be given when we look at the phenomenon from a linguistic *and* social perspective' (emphasis in original).[14] The analysis of social processes and institutions remains conceptually and methodologically separate from the analysis of language, even when the language is seen as encapsulated in the social framework (e.g. education is seen as 'an institution whose meanings are linguistically expressed'[15]). While recognising that the semantic analysis of communication, i.e. of the communicative role of language used by actors, can only be accomplished by a recognition of the social roles of actors, both Hasan and Kress display a certain ambiguity which tends to obscure what they set out to do. They seek to approach language in such a way that, as Kress puts it, they emphasise 'the total connectedness of linguistic and social processes'[16] but nonetheless sometimes speak as if they wanted to approach language from the outside by bringing a separate social analysis to it, and proceeding to ideology critique through the *correlation* of social structure and language forms. For Kress, most contemporary linguistic theories are silent about 'how texts are read and heard'[17] or the reasons for writing and speaking. So the forms of language must be explored by a comparative and cross-cultural analysis of the occurrence of forms which reveals their function. Hasan's approach is similar.

I do not wish to argue that the critical use of systemics has been mistaken or unfruitful, quite the contrary. Systemics has provided a great deal of insight into language and communication. But it has only recently explicitly developed a strategy which is the strategy with which Habermas begins — the *internal* development of a critical dimension within linguistic theory. In this strategy it would not be considered sufficient to speak of the 'connectedness' of the social process and language forms because it is argued that language is inherently social in precisely the critical sense that Hasan and Kress (and Halliday) want to convey.

I think it would be doing an injustice to Kress and Hasan to suggest that they do not hold the view that actors contest definitions of situations and their roles in them, and that this internal dimension of communication has critical potential. The problem I have identified may be the sort of problem that arises for pioneers whose contributions develop over time and are spread out over many works. As the theory develops, shifts of meaning and emphasis occur which sometimes lead to infelicitous ways of putting things. Habermas has notoriously had problems of this kind, too. It may also be a problem of 'audience' since the bulk of the linguistic community has had to be dragged from structural linguistics into pragmatics and still has some problems with the idea of language as a social semiotic.

These problems appear to show up in Hasan's view of ideology[18] which is ambiguous. In some places she speaks of it as if it were 'fashions of speaking' and 'habitual forms of communication', a view quite close to that adopted here. But it is formally defined as '... a socially constructed system of ideas which appears inevitable', and she speaks of language as a transmitter of ideological content. The general thrust of her analysis of mother–child talk is consistent with this latter emphasis on content rather than structure, although the analysis is pushed in the direction of structure when she endorses a concept of ideological 'codes' (in Bernstein's sense). It is *what* mothers say that is ideological: 'Mummy is silly!', 'I *have* to get Daddy's dinner now'. It is consistent with this content emphasis for Hasan to feel it necessary to emphasise that for an ideology to exist it must 'permeate' daily life, coming from the outside *into* the home and mother–child talk.

The difference between the permeation of daily life by a system of ideas (content) and by a set of practices which constrains subjects in speaking so that particular forms of self-representation *seem* to articulate their real situations, is an important difference. Is ideology found primarily in practices of structuration (of meaning making), in which socially created and sustained categories of people are constrained to make meanings and self-meaning, in particular ways, through 'habitual ways of speaking', with systems of ideas a by-product of this everyday life process, *or*, are the structures of speaking the product of sets of meanings? Do we use metaphors of penetration or permeation and see the presence of ideology in daily life as needing explanation or do we use some metaphor of dissemination (birth?) from daily life into grander public reifications, such as intellectuals produce? Perhaps a dialectical approach to this question would satisfy some, but I am inclined to the view that the structures of interaction are primary, although the products of past structuration are a constraint and resource for present processes. I wish to adopt this emphasis because I want to see the content of ideology as historically changing and flexible, while the usages of power go on forever.

If this view is adopted, it is no longer seen as surprising that ideology penetrates daily life. On the contrary, ideology is a part of daily life. It penetrates science and philosophy, and that is, technically speaking, surprising, given the pretensions to objectivity of some views of science and philosophy. If this view of the origins of ideology is adopted, then the other characteristic that Hasan identifies is no longer surprising — its taken-for-grantedness. What we then have to do is achieve an understanding of the particular ideological apparatuses (to coin a phrase) which impose such practices on daily life. These apparatuses are *not* systems of ideas but material conditions of ownership of mass media, legally supported constraints on speaking subjects (e.g. management prerogatives, supervisory practices, staff appraisal) and other concrete communicative practices.

Hasan's ideology critique is troubled by a wavering of viewpoint from one which is internal to one which is *external* to her linguistics. Ideology 'permeates'[19] daily life, language is an 'expression'[20] of ideology. I would prefer ideology to be an expression of language and critique to be something that does not spring from externally applying a supposedly non-ideological system of ideas to criticise speech habits. I want to avoid the problem of justification that arises when I seek to claim that my system of ideas about men and women, children and teachers is non-ideological and so permits me to point out ideologies from 'on high'. If I can find a basis for critique that is both content-free (in the special sense of content concerning the subject matter of norms) and internal to language, I will have avoided this burden. The subjects themselves can make their own, immanent critique. That is what Habermas' theory of the *methodology* of valid critique seeks to do.

6 Situations and Critique

Analysing Situated Talk Structures (Genres)

It is at the level of context of situation that we make decisions to construct communication in terms of particular assumed world relations and sets of assumptions about learners. In this chapter we will examine some concrete examples of the influence of context on text and the ways in which their awareness of the alternative and ideal features of speech might affect participation by pupils. In addition to the overt display of social distance in talk, there is a covert variation in role distance — the degree to which participants accept their agent roles or merely, perhaps, play them; this is related closely to motivation and learning. Participation is a two-level process. Overt participation does not necessarily imply role acceptance. Sooner or later the participant whose heart is not in it becomes bored and 'distant'. Perhaps that is why the overwhelming emotion reported by even academically able students in their final years of secondary school is boredom.

There is a close relationship between the types of validity claim participants are oriented to in the ISS and Halliday's aspects of context of situation. However, just as Halliday's set of functions doesn't quite fit function typologies of other linguists[1] and cannot itself be decisively justified, so Habermas' typology of validity questions does not quite fit into Halliday's functional categories. The relationship between the two seems to be as follows:

Habermas		*Halliday*
Truth claims	raised through	Existential functions
Rightness ⎱ Truthfulness ⎰	raised through	Interpersonal functions
Intelligibility ⎱ Aptness etc. ⎰	(possibly) raised through	Textual functions

The existential realisation of field relations of *speech-in-a-relationship* (remember, the functions are always co-present) are inevitably cast as *claims* because they are reality references made by one person to another in a purposive

73

situation to which such 'facts' are relevant. The linguist/observer cannot bracket out the existential implication of an utterance as if utterances were equivalent to philosophically disembodied 'propositions'. That would be to treat them as if they were part of *another* language game — that played by logicians. Errors of this kind are often made in the name of objectivity. Conversely, those who wish to keep the whole, situated and mutually conditioning set of meanings together are often accused of committing the naturalistic fallacy — confusing fact and value. In a way, that is just what manipulative use of speech in classrooms seeks to get a hearer to do; accept something as a fact, because the context/source is valued.

Let us take a common example of a relatively uncontroversial genre, the 'service encounter'. The first example is drawn from Halliday and Hasan's *Language, Context and Text*:[2]

C: Can I have ten oranges and a kilo of bananas please?
V: Yes, anything else?
C: No, thanks.
V: That'll be a dollar forty.
C: Two dollars.
V: Sixty, eighty, two dollars. Thank you.

The contextual configuration, the values of field, tenor and mode, is represented in abbreviated form as follows:

Field: Economic transaction: purchase of retail goods: perishable food.
Tenor: Agents of transaction: hierarchic: customer superordinate; social distance: near maximum.
Mode: Language role: ancillary; channel: phonic; medium: spoken with visual contact.

This, together with background cultural knowledge, about fruit and vegetable shops, permits a prediction along the lines of:

Sales Request: Can I have ... etc.
Sale Compliance: Yes, anything else?
                   No, thanks.
Sale: That'll be $$ x ... (where price calculation by weight is necessary)
Purchase: Two dollars. (Gives too much money)
Purchase Closure: Sixty, eighty ... (Gives change)

These are all obligatory elements in the expected pattern, although they may be realised in many ways: for example, the customer simply proffers the two dollars without speaking. They are coded as: SR^SC^S^P^PC (where ^

indicates fixed sequence between compulsory elements). The explanation of one element here can serve to show how the analysis might run:

> I shall use the term SALE COMPLIANCE irrespective of whether the response is positive or negative. In [the text] SC is positive ... It is important to realise that *yes* is not meant as just a short form for *Yes, you can have ten oranges* ...; rather, it is an encouraging noise that says *Yes, go on! Ask for more things.* ... Its prime purpose is sales promotion ... Behind the invitation to buy some more lies the ideology of 'free enterprise' ...[3]

Whether a free enterprise ideology is involved or not, one might well believe that a closer and more mundane calculation of self-interest may also be involved. Presumably shopkeepers in Babylon made similar moves, since it is usually in the interests of those who sell for a profit to increase their sales. (Although 'bargaining' is realised in a different genre from that presently under discussion, this particular move may occur in several genres.) The question the customer, no doubt from time immemorial, has considered at this point in the genre is whether he or she *really* wants anything else.

The next textual example in Halliday and Hasan's book adds in some of the optional components of the genre. The above obligatory components seem to be those that are necessary to achieve the mechanics of a sale/purchase. They are, to a degree, realisations of communicative functions that are predictable from situation and culture: if you want something in a shop that sells many things, you must indicate what you want, if not by speech by pointing or some other means; you must know the price, if not by price tag, by asking; you must pay, if not the exact amount, then you may be entitled to receive change, and so on. Let's look at other ways the genre might go:

V: Yes, anything else?
C: I wanted some strawberries but these don't look very ripe.
V: O they're ripe all right. I tried some myself ...

But the salesperson might be telling lies in the pursuit of a sale. No doubt experienced customers are aware of such possibilities:

C: Let me try one.

If the strawberries are as sour as they look, the salesperson's claim may come under doubt. Perhaps it was a lie. If so, it would be an example of perlocutionary linguistic action. The trusting customer, in the meantime, could have still been proceeding in an illocutionary way, seeking simply to establish the state of ripeness of the strawberries and expecting the salesperson to co-operate in that. A wise shopkeeper might well reason that a happy customer is one who will buy strawberries again and so see a coincidence of interests in establishing the real state of the strawberries. Such a person might well have responded to the original doubts about ripeness with an invitation to try one. In the innocent setting of the fruit shop we may still encounter differences of interest and manipulative uses of language as well as resistance to manipulation. What is interesting about the non-standard development of this service encounter, and about the optional components of a genre generally, is that the alternative possibilities revealed in these tell us a great deal about the core genre — the obligatory components. While the optional components may not define genre species, they may be crucial in analysing the critical potential of them.

The generic structure of the shopping example has certain points at which the potential for manipulation is greatest. If we consider what Hasan calls the 'agent roles' in terms of common and complementary interests they may be seen as reciprocal and complementary roles — the vendor has something to sell and the customer has something they want to buy. But if we consider the agent roles in terms of both convergent and *divergent* interests, it is possible to identify points in the dialogue structure (which is also an action structure involving concrete buying and selling) at which differences of interest emerge.

Similarly, Hasan's assumption that the relationship in the sales encounter is hierarchically biased in favour of the buyer ('the vendor is in a soliciting position, having to sell the goods')[4] is not necessarily true of all sales encounters. It depends on whether it is a buyer's or a seller's market. The training of sales people in the door to door selling industry has often been based on teaching them to take a highly active and controlling role in sales encounters. This often involves giving the illusion that it is a seller's market ('There is only one left!'; 'This offer closes tomorrow!' etc.) or involves manipulation of the tenor to create the illusion of a personal rather than a sales/soliciting relationship ('Look, I'm going to do you a favour, Bill'). Sophisticated consumers may well be relatively immune to all this, but there is also an endless supply of 'suckers' or 'punters', since such techniques are still among those taught to sales staff in some industries.

The first and obvious point of possible divergence of interests in the sales encounter is that at which the vendor seeks to generate further sales requests after the first one. In the car industry it is sometimes in the generation of the sale of 'options' and gimmicks after the basic sale of the car has been completed. It is possible to assume, as Hasan points out, that this iteration might be predicted on the basis of two assumptions:

1. the customer does not remember all the goods (he or she came into the shop to buy) at once and/or
2. the vendor must display readiness to serve and continue to invite more SRs.[5]

While such assumptions may fit the fruit shop example reasonably well, they construct the encounter as one in which only convergent interests operate. But you could equally assume that the vendor seeks more SRs in order to increase sales and thereby to maximise profits. This is in the vendor's interest but not *necessarily* in the customer's.

A second point of this kind is located at the Sale ('That'll be a dollar forty'). In the aforementioned Babylonian shop, it might well have been the case that there were no fixed prices. The vendor may have based the price on a shrewd appraisal of what the customer might be able to afford to pay. In the modern antiques trade, this is called 'ramping'. If we construct the agent roles as convergent, we might not be alert to these possibilities.

To sum up, the vendor has an interest in maximising profit. This can be done by selling more items or charging higher prices. Whether the vendor takes a long-term or short-term view of maximising profit will depend on the likelihood of repeat business, the vendor's personal plans and so on. Clearly, an itinerant street pedlar may view things differently from one's neighbourhood fruit vendor of ten years' acquaintanceship. Only in the latter case is there any substantial area of common interest.

It is thus possible, given some background knowledge, to label some of the points in a genre where manipulative potential based on divergence of interests may exist. In addition to the formula for generic structure potential (GSP) one might devise a formula for manipulative structure potential (MSP). A general symbol for such points in a generic structure might be (!). If so, the full GSP for the sales encounter might be rewritten:

$$[(G.(SI)^\wedge)][(SE.<)\{SR^\wedge SC^\wedge!\}^\wedge S!]P^\wedge PC(^\wedge F)$$

(Don't worry about the technical details for the moment!)

One might expect, across a large sample of sales encounters, to find the largest number of both general alignment devices, such as 'probe', 'repair' and 'realignment', and other manipulative devices deployed at these points of divergence of interests. This will be so because a buyer might not only have forgotten what they came to the shop for, but there may also be reasons of self-interest for buyers not wanting to make sales requests or to show any eagerness to buy at a stated price. Some codings, such as Hasan's, tend to obscure the possible presence of manipulative devices:

       --- C: I wanted some strawberries but these don't look ripe.
       [
    SE [V: O they're ripe all right. They're just that colour a
       [kinda greeny pink.

```
       [                [ -----------------------------------------------------------------
       [ C: Mm I see. [ Will they be O.K. for this evening?
       ------------------ [
    SE [ V: O yeah. They'll be fine. I had some yesterday and
       [ they're good very sweet and fresh.
       ---------------------------------------------------------------------------------
       SR [ - C: O all right then. I'll take two.⁶
```

Hasan's coding SE includes both the E (enquiry) and the response. This obscures the very interesting strategy of the vendor in replying to enquiries about the quality of goods offered for sale ('Never mind the quality feel the width'). Perhaps an alternative coding might be:

SE -- C: I wanted some strawberries but these don't *look* ripe.
DG -- V: O they're all right ...

where SE still stands for Sales Enquiry but DG stands for a particular type of response, called Defence of Goods. This usually follows the strategy of responding directly to the aspect of the goods called in question ('C: But it's such a dreadful colour. V: I tell you, it's so fashionable all the young things are wearing it'). Many other strategies are possible. With a timid customer, the vendor could go on the offensive ('What are you saying. When I go to the markets I don't buy the best?'); with another, excuses might serve ('It's too early in the season').

As they stand, when applied in any *given* sales situation, the categories developed in Hasan's examples of analysis of this genre run the risk of being seen as ideological, in the classical sense of obscuring the truth in the interests of some class or category of people. Similarly, talk of 'the' task or purpose of a genre assumes that there is a single, culturally recognised task involved. But there are as many or more tasks than participants, and the construction of a task situation as complementary (Task = you buy what I sell) may run the risk of privileging the culture of one class in society rather than another class or marginal groups.

The validity questions which arise are intimately intertwined with each other and with the differences of interests of the categories of speakers. Claims about the ripeness of the strawberries are at stake. But equally, normative claims that the shopkeeper makes on customers through the presence of norms of politeness (you can't call someone a liar to their face) and even specific norms that have built up in the relationship over time (Mr Smith likes his fruit to be just right and that's OK because he appreciates good fruit) are co-present and interacting with attempts to resolve the first type of claim about ripeness. Expressive claims made largely through non-verbal signs of sincerity or doubt are woven through the tapestry. The simultaneous resolution of all these claims in a socially acceptable manner would be a considerable exercise of communicative competence on the part of the customer, especially if the strawberries *were* green. However, this would not be made easy by the generic structure, which marshals the power of social convention and trust against the customer, assuming the customer is being less detached and machiavellian than the shopkeeper here. Indeed, to the extent that one party to the transaction is being machiavellian and the other sincere, the communicative process is distorted.

And the realisation of the elements in a genre structure is not simply a linguistic event but a social, political and economic event. The validity questions involved are not mere abstractions. They have real consequences. The generic expectations in a situation can result, as anyone who has done a bit of shopping will know, in advantage and disadvantage. There are points in the generic structure where clear divergence of interests may be identified and it is at these points that you find, as you might expect, apparatuses of repair and other, similar strategies coming into use to keep resisting communicators 'in play'. Again, as you might expect, it is the agent whose interests are immediately reflected in sticking to the generic expectations who seeks to bring the other party back into line, and the agent whose interests are not immediately reflected who might seek to breach the expectations. In the case of the sales encounter we may constitute the genre differently under different conditions of 'market power'. Under some circumstances the structural expectation of the GSP can be a force for exploitation and it is in the interests of the customer to break off communication or offer other kinds of resistance. In this way, both in the trivial example of the fruit shop, or in the not so trivial example of a family living below the poverty line seeking to buy an old car or rent a house, we may critically examine all genres.

The teaching and learning agent roles

Much the same sort of analysis may be made of different learning situations and related differences in the task or goal and the roles of the principal agent types, teachers and learners. Naturalistic and observational research on teaching, both behavioural and linguistic, has shown considerable convergence in its depiction of the task of the classroom (as defined by teachers, at least), and of the agent roles and the teaching/learning relationship in most of our schools, most of the time.

Smith and Geoffrey's[7] ethnographic study of urban classrooms summarised the tasks of the classroom as: to 'cover' the set curriculum, to achieve sufficient 'control' to make the pupils do this, and to ensure that they achieve a sufficient level of 'mastery' of the set curriculum, as revealed by evaluation. Observations of linguists have added that the set curriculum is expressed in its own (often technical) language, and mastery of this is a prerequisite to demonstrating mastery of the curriculum proper.[8] Still other observers have noted that the process is expected to happen by the teacher actively 'teaching' and that teacher talk constitutes about 75% of total 'official' talk in classrooms. Indeed, the need to use the word 'official' indicates that the linguistic regime of most classrooms is characterised by a total ban on all pupil talk except that specifically elicited by the teacher, although this ban is only sporadically enforced, even in the quietest classrooms.

This kind of classroom has been called the 'traditional' classroom, and there may be some reason to believe that the growth of group work and other methods which stress pupil activity has broken down the prevalence of the traditional pattern, although I have seen no systematic evidence of this. However, many researchers have reported that teachers often perceive themselves as offering pupils a chance to talk and express themselves but that this perception is not supported by observation.

In the present argument, this kind of classroom has been called the method classroom, because, it is argued, the pattern observed there stems from the combination of a curriculum built around a mistaken idea of the nature of the method of inquiry, and a pedagogy which is the expression of a related mistake about how learning occurs. The pedagogy of the method classroom expresses itself in a set of textual forms which express the context of situation characteristic of the method classroom. A recent study by a student in the Primary Bachelor of Education programme at the University of Sydney, K. A. Gambley,[9] identified different forms of the elementary school classroom 'show and tell' or 'news session' (where children tell about things and events from outside the official curriculum). The data collected in this study exemplify both the dominant classroom context type and departures from it of a more discursive kind.

Three teachers self-taped the 'news session' lessons in their classrooms over a period of time. A random selection was made from each set and analysed closely. Each teacher was also interviewed about her goals and aims in this type of lesson. Three different genres of 'news' were identified, one for each classroom, with all tapes from that classroom conforming generically. A caveat: the set of three certainly cannot be regarded as exhausting the possible generic variation of 'news sessions'. In addition, the identification of them as separate genres is dependent on the application of Hasan's concept of genre and the development of typology at a high level of delicacy.

Compare three text sections in which a child recounts a birthday experience. Before exploring the nature of the field, let us begin with some aspects of the variations in tenor observed by Gambley (Table 2).

TABLE 2 *Variations in tenor in three classroom texts*

	Text 1	Text 2	Text 3
Agent role relation	hierarchic	less hierarchic	minimal hierarchy
Social distance	near maximal	less social distance	minimal social distance

Now let us look at the texts one by one before returning to the specification of field.

Text 1

T:	Could you put that in your bag? Good morning Elizabeth.
P:	Good morning, Mrs. Fowler.
T:	Any news?
{ **P:**	Yes please.
{ **P:**	I've got a cold.
P:	Good morning girls and boys.
P:	Good morning, Elizabeth.
P:	It's my daddy's birthday.
T:	Today? What did he get for his birthday?
P:	Flowers, chocolate, and from my mum ... he got umm ... he he he ... umm ... he was waiting for a very large thing so what we did is I raced in to him and said ... and I raced and I said dad to race to the garage and get his new bike, and when he saw it he couldn't believe his eyes 'cause he he forgot it was his birthday.
T:	My goodness, and who gave him the flowers?
P:	Me.
T:	Oh, how beautiful! What sort of flowers, do you know what they were? What were they called?
P:	Roses.
T:	Oh, roses. One of my favourite flowers!
simult.[**P:**	The rose garden.
simult.[**P:**	And they were they were pink ...
T:	And my favourite colour, ohhh ... Okay, thank you, Elizabeth. umm, good morning, Nicholas ...

This pattern is typical for this teacher. Each news giving involves extensive teacher questioning and evaluative comments ('how beautiful', etc.) on student answers, then a brisk move on to the next pupil. The teacher's questions are gererally concrete and 'closed'. The whole class watches each time while the teacher interacts with one pupil.

Text 2

T: Can you tell us about today, Sarah?
P: It was my birthday.
T: Today?
P: No, last night.
T: And can you tell us about it, what happened?
P: Well, I had so many people! I had Cassie ... Put your hand up if you came to my birthday ... All them people.
T: And did you have a good time?
P: Yeah.
P: Stephen, you weren't there.
P: Yes, we were.
T: Yes.
P: Somebody gave me a musical book? Jennifer.
T: And can you tell us about your musical book. [the class is interrupted by a late pupil]
P: Guess what kind guess what kind my cake was.
T: I don't know.
P: Chocolate.

Here the child news teller plays a more active role, calling on a show of hands, asking the teacher to guess, but the teacher is still guiding the process by questioning. A greater proportion of this teacher's questions are relatively 'open', e.g.

'What did you do?'
'Johnny?' (invitation to tell anything he likes)

Text 3

P: Umm, guess what I did?
[**T:** ... I can't guess..
[**P:** I we had Pascale and me had birthday cake for her birthday.
T: Whereabouts? At Pascale's place?
P: My place.
T: Your place? Oh, isn't that lovely. Tell me some of the things Pascale.
P: Umm ... yucky cream cake!
T: Yucky cream cake? Isn't it *wonderful* cream cake?
P: It was yucky. We hate cream cake.

T: Do you. Why?
P: Because.
P: We like chocolate cream cake.
T: And they forgot to make it chocolate, did they?

The children in this classroom also have the opportunity to ask questions and take the initiative, but the teacher's moves take on more of the quality of a conversation, as contrasted with text 2 where the more teacherly request to 'tell about' is common.

Other texts of the latter two teachers show more sustained and less routine treatment of topics than the teacher of text 1. They are also characterised by more child/child interaction, comment and so on (as a part of the news session rather than a disruption to it), and pupil questioning of pupil news givers for purposes of clarification.

One transcript from classroom 3 (chosen at random) shows that teacher talk as a proportion of lines of typescript is only 35%, whereas one of classroom 1's transcripts chosen at random shows that teacher talk is over 50%, and this in a session where children are supposed to be telling *their* news. An interview with teacher 1 revealed a view of the goals of the lesson which corresponded with the textual evidence. Teacher 1 was interested in building self-esteem, and discussed pedagogy in terms of the teacher's role in manipulating the hypothetical internal pupil constructs of cognitive/behavioural psychology, such as self-concept. This teacher was unaware that her linguistic practices might constrain pupils' talk in ways that directly contradict her stated goals. She spoke of her practice of the news session as a means to other educational goals of a psychological kind, rather than in terms of her pupils' possible goals.

As long ago as 1916 Dewey had a great deal to say about this kind of teaching. Speaking of the nature of a community, Dewey warns:

> ... within even the most social group there are many relations which are not as yet social. A large number of human relations in any social group are still upon the mechanical plane. Individuals use one another so as to get desired results ... so far as the relations of parent and child, teacher and pupil remain on this level, they form no true social group ... giving and taking of orders modifies action and results, but does not of itself effect a sharing of purposes, a communication of interests.[10]

The other two teachers appeared to define the task differently. Instead of a methodical operation on children's psyches, the task was defined as an opportunity for them to develop through doing something themselves. The means of this was the creation of a conversation which the children are invited to join, but which is still guided by the teacher. The first teacher created a task defined in terms of methods of bringing about caused events of a developmental kind by teacher manipulation of processes; the second and third, a task defined in terms of facilitating a process whereby the pupils themselves would, by their own self-transcending efforts, bring about their own development.

Any specification of the field of situation 1 would have to identify the task of teaching as defined by this teacher. But what is the task of learning in such a classroom? Clearly, rather a passive or receptive one.

The complexities of the Generic Structure Potential (GSP) formulae for the three genres, as set out by Gambley in her thesis, do not concern us here, but some aspects of differences in compulsory elements are worth attention. To give the flavour of the analysis: in classroom 1, the structure is simpler, and pupil news giving is a compulsory element, which follows the teacher's News Invitation and is followed by (typically) teacher's (evaluative) comment. In contrast, in classroom 3, the teacher's News Invitation may be followed by News Giving, but the sequence may also begin with a child's News Offer. After News Giving, other children's questions and comments, followed by News Extension is common. What was an obligatory component in the first classroom becomes an alternative, and therefore optional, component in the other two. The task of the news in these classrooms appears to involve a more active role for both the news giver, who may volunteer, and for pupils other than the news giver, who have only the role of audience in classroom 1.

But where would we put the exclamation marks (!) in these examples? What are the interests of the children which are at stake in the news session? We may have to do a bit of guessing here. Perhaps we can tap into the world of these children's interests by remembering our own childhood. Who came to our parties? Who had better presents than we did? Who had a chocolate cake? What disappointments brought us to tears and what joys delighted us? There is little chance to pursue any of these agendas in classroom 1. There you must stick to the official version of reality and avoid dangerous ground. Not nearly so exciting or envy-making as having all those who came to your party raise their hands in class! Of course, there is room here for the teacher as senior partner in the dialogue to reflect upon morals and manners, that is, on the normative claims in the talk, but at least the world of childhood gets into more interesting territory in classrooms 2 and 3. There, the children get to pursue agendas of their own to some extent, which means getting a chance to solve their own problems. The critical theoretical question is just this: how open is a situation to the expression of the interests of all categories of participants? Our earlier discussion of motivation should have made it clear that this is not unconnected with how interesting the situation is in the other sense of the word 'interest'.

An example of the very stuff of childhood life from classroom 3:

T: At recess I noticed that Fred was being very very nice. Very caring. He was concerned about someone. Can anyone tell me what I mean by being caring and concerned?

P: Get him an iceblock?

T: Who?

P: Fred gave John an iceblock.

T: Oh. Why did Fred do that?

F: Because I like him. He's my friend.

T: Uhuh. Why do you like him? Cause he's in year three isn't he. He's a big kid.

F: Yeah. Yeah, 'cause he lets me play with his toys.

T: Yeah. Any other reason?

F: Yes.

T: Mmm?

F: Why do I play with him? 'cause 'cause last time when I met him he didn't know me very well ...

T: Right. And you think if you play together ...

F: Yeah.

T: ... you'll get to know each other.

F: Yep. Better.

Questions where a teacher asks a pupil why, when the action or problem about which the why is being asked are the pupil's, have a clear potential for helping the pupil to make the elements of their own problem clearer to themselves and so contribute towards better problem solving. The teacher here is also modelling a skill which is the beginning of the process of universalisation — the process of understanding another in an explicit way.

Where pupil/pupil talk is not emerging or is confined to sequential calling out of the answers to a teacher question, for example

P: I'll choose someone.

P: I'll take you.

P: Me too

it can be deliberately structured to create new types of pupil move:

T: Bonnie will speak next and Omar will ask questions for what she says.

although I would not recommend imitating one teacher who practised this (described by Roth[11]), who also insisted on the questions asked being the same sort as teachers so often ask to see if children are listening or not:

P: [after telling about an event] What was I doing, Sandy?

S: Dancing.

P: No.
P2: Chasing?
P: Oh, yes.

In contrasting show and tell (news) sessions she observed, Roth comes to much the same conclusions from her impressionistic approach as Gambley did from a systemic analysis:

> The activity seems to be more child-centered in [one classroom type] that is, more open to the personal knowledge of students. In [the other type] ... there is more of a tendency to direct attention away from the child toward a display of the ability to form questions that the teacher considers 'good' or the ability to repeat the information stated ... This preference gives the activity a testlike, impersonal quality.[12]

For 'impersonal' read 'thing-like' and you have come close to the ontological issue again.

The point about interest is reinforced by Roth's analysis of post-lesson interviews with pupils. One child who resisted the requirement to ask questions said afterwards that she feigned ignorance of what to ask because 'I get tired of making up questions'. Another child displayed anger during the interview because she had missed her turn to speak. Her relationships were what interested her, not the content of what was told as News: 'It was my turn, not Omar's!' Still another explained why he tried to sabotage the process by spelling instead of saying his answers: 'I was just trying to have some fun.'

Again we see that the disconnection from the real interests of pupils is also a disconnection from motivation:

Researcher: Why were you reading all through Show and Tell?
Pupil: Sometimes I get tired of it.
Researcher: Of what?
Pupil: Of it all!
Researcher: All of what?
Pupil: Just *all* of it![13]

Abnormal Communication Characterises Classrooms

The two basic classroom types, method and discourse, are characterised by different values of field and tenor. In them, teachers and, insofar as they follow, pupils, have a different definition of task and teaching/learning relationship. The two different basic types of context of situation relate to that distinction between 'mechanical' and 'communicative' that Dewey employed. Whatever the personal attitudes of the teachers concerned, we are speaking here of their professional thinking and their teaching method. The issue is not one of black hats and white hats, but of definitions of the educational task and the teaching role. The discourse classroom is characterised by what Dewey called 'normal communication', which he distinguished from mechanical communication in a manner very like Habermas' distinction between communicative and strategic action. Normal communication is the kind you find between friends and colleagues in everyday life, mechanical communication is essentially communication as manipulation:

> By normal communication is meant that in which there is a joint interest, a common interest, so that one is eager to give and the other to take. It contrasts with telling or stating things simply for the sake of impressing them on another, merely in order to test him to see how much he has retained and can literally reproduce.[14]

It is not surprising that the teacher in classroom 1 reported that she and the children often felt bored during the dutiful recounting of news in her classroom. The basic type of the classroom context of situation is closely related to the motivational type that is fostered there. Teachers in general report that the problem of interesting the pupils is the greatest educational problem they face after they have made some headway with the problem of control, which is the number one problem in the first few years of teaching. Typically, the problem-solving strategy of teachers is to look for new pedagogical tricks to capture children's interest. But, then, most classrooms are method classrooms. Whatever the failures of alternative schools and 'open education', lack of interest by pupils does not loom nearly so large as a problem in them. The solution to the problem of interest is a new relationship of interest*s*, not a technical fix.

The two classroom types are an outworking of context, as defined by our culture and its conception of teaching. The method classroom is one in which teachers objectify learners and reify knowledge, drawing on a body of objectifying knowledge and pedagogy constructed by the behavioural sciences for the former and empiricist and related understandings of knowledge for the latter. In the discourse classroom we find the learner as pedagogical partner, rather than pedagogical object. The pedagogy is consciously co-constructed (instead of unconsciously, as in the method classroom). Pedagogy is not something teachers alone plan, but learning strategies children are given room for — in a structured way. Some teachers seem to be able to do this more or less instinctively but others have to work slowly towards it out of a growing awareness of a late twentieth-century understanding of the humanness and historicity of knowledge and the nature of our global problems. The difference in tenor between one teaching/learning situation and another may be located on a dimension from the child as educational or learning object (that is, treated by the teacher, professionally or pedagogically, as an object which learns) to the child as co-inquirer. Dewey's compromise is somewhere in the middle. The difference in field may be stretched out along a dimension from the notion of the classroom task as the input or telling of information, to be reproduced, to the notion of it as drawing the child into the great conversations of the species, and facilitating the active autopoetic principle of the child's development.

Classroom communication which is so constrained that pupils cannot respond rationally to claims but are confined to producing 'correct' forms of answers to fit into teacher frameworks is bad communication from the stand-point of evolutionary education. The reasons for this should by now have become clear. First, if correct answers can be supplied by rote or lower order cognitive processes and in a manner tied closely to a particular context, pupils fail to achieve curriculum goals of understanding and generality. Second, it is bad communication because a rote response does not in itself assist the develop-ment of reasoning and problem-solving skills. Third, because there is no oppor-tunity to develop social skills and practise the courage required in argument. Fourth, because there is little room in such communication for the interplay between the hazy glimpse of the final shape of an argument, and the present stage of it, that is a necessary part of all creative rationality. Fifth, it is bad com-munication because it inculcates distorted habits of response in which, unable to respond to truth claims as such, pupils respond instead to the teacher's authority. Sixth, because the pupil's self-valuation as a rational being is jeopardised by being treated as an object of pedagogy rather than a partner in inquiry. Seventh, because it does not allow those who have the closest knowledge of the pupils' learning difficulties, the pupils themselves, the opportunity to express and explore those difficulties. Eighth, because it militates against the conditions required for the universalisation of problem solving, namely the chance of reflecting on our own beliefs and values that interaction on an equal footing with others who see things differently can give us.

The choice for teachers is simple enough. Teacher utterances are a manifold claim. Either the relational claim that a teacher makes on a learner is completely and ubiquitously dominant, to the detriment of other validity claims, or the claims of the pupil as an apprentice co-inquirer are given some weight and the relational claim of cognitive authority and trust that the teacher may make is made with restraint. Either the pupil will be a pedagogical object or a developing fellow citizen of our one world.

7 Genre and Classroom Type

The Roles of Questions in Teaching

The transformation of the pupil into a pedagogical object means the creation of an object which has to be tested in order to ascertain whether various manipulations have been successful. This may be contrasted with situations where there is a great deal of common purpose, to use Dewey's phrase. In the method classroom, the most that can be achieved is common *extrinsic* or strategic purpose — the interlacing of the egocentric calculations of actors — and this for only a proportion of the student body. You see this sort of purpose in learning when you talk to academically able middle-class pupils in our schools. They don't talk a lot about intrinsic motivation, about loving the subject and their fascination for or interest in it. They talk a lot about getting the grades they want or need. The coincidence of their desire to achieve and the teacher's to teach is accidental as far as the subject matter is concerned. Indeed, in the competitive statistically scaled matriculation system in New South Wales, where some subjects are rumoured to gain a scaling boost from statistical manipulation of the marks, some students choose subjects on the basis of likely marks as much, or more than, on the basis of suitability for later studies or liking for the subject. Common intrinsic purpose is much rarer.

The two types of classrooms will display a different range of contexts of situation and, insofar as questioning plays a role in them, a different set of roles for questioning. The two classroom types may be contrasted along dimensions of field and tenor in the following way:

Tenor

P: pupil as learning object   pupil as subject of learning

|———————————————————————————————————|

T: teacher as teller   teacher as guide

Field

P: practising, listening, reproducing   doing, stating, theorising

|———————————————————————————————————|

T: telling, testing, task setting   raising questions, facilitating

The agent roles of teacher and pupil form complementary pairs which differ from one classroom type to another and from situation type to situation type within each classroom type.

To help us model the variation in pupil role, we might use the analogy of a traveller in a strange land. The traveller is learning the language and customs by meeting people and situations. The citizens of this land may adopt two differing strategies when they meet such a traveller: they may be tolerant of the traveller's attempts to learn their language and forgiving for any breaches of custom committed, or they may feel that the traveller should not wander until they can speak the language well and must be held strictly responsible for their breaches of custom. In the first case, the traveller might be permitted to ask questions, even to ask them badly. When they seem to be behaving wrongly, the citizens might well ask travellers questions concerning what it is they are trying to do. In the second case, there will be little attempt to make allowances. Itineraries will be set up so the travellers get a controlled view of the country and any questions from them will be discouraged. Does this all sound rather familiar? With this kind of contrast in mind, let us look a little more closely at the many functions questions can play.

Questions are a very important part of classroom discourse. More than 80 years of classroom research has shown the persistence of questioning as a favourite teacher methodology. Researchers since Romiette Stevens' pioneering study of 1912 have noted this and have deplored that so many questions are asked (roughly 60% of all classroom talk), that nearly all are asked by teachers and that so many of them require only a rote answer (possibly as many as 90% when coding problems in earlier studies are taken into account). Stevens complained: 'The fact that one teacher has the ability to quiz his pupils at the rate of two or three questions a minute is a matter of comparatively slight importance; the fact that one hundred classrooms reveal the same methods in vogue is quite another matter.'[1]

The educational problem with questions, as Stevens recognised, lies in the effect on the pupil. Do they encourage 'self-reliant, independent thinkers' (Stevens) or do they stress superficial judgement and memory above all else? Let us look more closely at this activity, on which teachers spend more than half their classroom time.

When is a question not a question?

The answer to this question is: when the question is already an answer ... or a statement ... or a warning ... or a message ... or ... almost anything.

The confusion of surface forms with function, coupled with simplistic understandings of function, has long bedevilled analysis of classroom talk. The fact that a teacher's utterance has some sort of interrogative grammatical form does not mean that it is functionally 'a question' or that it is a particular 'kind' of question, for example open, closed or rhetorical.

What are we to make, then, of generations of studies of classroom talk which have been informed by only the most primitive notions of context and which present as their most significant findings quantitative analyses of teacher/pupil questioning behaviour — studies, for instance, of 'open-ended questions' and their role, which try to correlate percentages of open-ended teacher questions in a sample of classrooms with pupil outcomes? From the standpoint of modern pragmatics, such studies are hopelessly misconceived. Even if 'open-endedness' were a viable functional concept, question forms could never be unequivocally assigned to the category on the basis of the *form* of interrogative utterances. It is for this reason that the usually reported 80% of teacher questions as questions which call for a rote or memorised answer is probably an underestimate. Function is a product of contextualised interpretation by participants. Form is only one clue to this: the very least that would be necessary for the employment of functional categories would be an analysis of the whole structure in which individual utterances are embedded. Pupil answers, too, might tell you something about the function of particular teacher questions. Questions apparently 'open' in form (e.g. 'what were the causes of the Civil War?'), if here we equate open with admitting of a variety of possible acceptable answers, are functionally closed if, in the context, it is intended by the teacher, and taken by the students, to be the case that the question is really: 'What are the five causes of the Civil War ... in your textbook ... that I gave you in your notes last week ... etc.?' Quantitative studies which employ the impressionistic categorisation procedures common in behavioural science, working from either observation or transcripts, do not provide the accurate data on differences in rates of questioning types on which further quantitative comparisons of pupil learning depend. Many apparently 'open' questions are really 'closed' — functionally.

In any case, the concept pair 'open/closed' is not an open and shut case. Almost all talk proceeds in the light of some interpretive and structural expectations by participants. In a sense, almost all questions are 'closed' in some ways, and in all ways to some extent. A question might be relatively 'open' in one way (the teacher really intends the pupil to give a personal opinion of the causes of the Civil War) but 'closed' in other ways (the teacher expects 'the causes' to be drawn from the collection of historical causes already discussed in connection with previously studied historical events — economic, political, demographic, cultural or psychological). Any student (in most classrooms) who starts to talk about Divine Providence, or God's Judgement on the People of Athens, to tap just one (generally) forbidden view of cause in human history, would soon find out that the question wasn't 'open' in *every* respect.

Much the same problems afflict the descriptive research of many observational studies of classroom communication, although some of the broad conclusions of this work remain valid. (We can say, for instance, with some degree of confidence, that teachers ask the greater proportion of classroom questions (of whatever kind) and the pupils combined ask perhaps only one question for every eight to ten teacher questions, and so on.) But to go beyond this level we need to begin to think in terms of the way communication works. To enter this new territory we need a theory of language function. To raise educational issues, we need a critical theory of language function — a theory of communicative action.

Classroom communication is generally a highly structured area of human communication — at least, in 'good' or orderly classrooms of the kind that magically appear most times researchers with tape recorders arrive in them. Such classroom communication is strongly rule-governed, with regular structures of turn-taking,[2] and regular or predictable narrative and interactive forms. Meanings are co-produced or co-constructed by participants in context-specific ways. Context itself is constructed and signalled in classroom interaction in part through 'contextualisation cues'.[3] 'Functionally speaking' is speaking in terms of the purposes being publicly (i.e. linguistically) pursued by participants in the course of meaningful (usually goal-oriented) actions. That is why the way pupils 'take' teacher questions can be judged from, among other things, their answering strategies,[4] and it is why, in a classroom where the communication process seems orderly to the teacher, that way of taking the questions *is* their function. To understand what is going on, we need to know how teachers intend their questions to be 'taken' and how pupils 'take' them. We need to identify the structural expectations or 'procedural knowledge' of participants and to describe the structures that actually emerge — to describe them functionally, not just at a surface level. This means we cannot, for instance, be content with the identification of interrogative surface forms, but must identify functionally different types of questions.

The 'co-operative' character of classrooms does not mean that participants are necessarily conscious of co-operating to produce orderly talk in them. However, the co-operation which is necessary for any talk to be orderly can be of different kinds. It can be a product of an imposed framework, controlled and cued by one category of participant, or it can be a more precarious but ultimately more productive order which is the product of talk of the conversational type, which is genuinely co-operative in the classroom process as a shared responsibility for validity. The way questions work will also exhibit this difference. Only where there is in some sense a mutual readiness to understand others and to question one's own views can the preconditions for social and, potentially, universal problem solving exist.

In addition, we cannot be content with atomic analysis of utterances in isolation. We must look at utterances interactively. Questions are defined, progressively, by the way people answer them, by the questioners reaction to that, and by the upshot of that reaction contributing to the way the next question functions, and so on. We need to look at functionally relevant features of structure. It is at this level that the nature of the epistemic problematic of the talk becomes evident and we can recognise who it is whose problems are being addressed in the talk.

Erickson and Schultz, in their essay 'When is a Context?' make this latter point very clear:

> ... social behaviour [is] hierarchically organized from large slots down to small imbedded slots of microsecond duration ... Social performance ... can be apprehended ... as relationships of succession across time ... 'slots' of activity of short duration ... are strung together in interaction like beads in succession across time ... reduced by a *plan* into a simpler order ... but, because interaction is not an object but a social accomplishment ... it is as if all participants in interaction collectively create and sustain [it in the] mutually constructive interplay between expectation and action ...[5]

They go on to argue that this property of interaction requires that it be studied through the use of

> ... empirically derived models of the organization of interactional performance with emphasis on the principal parts of [social] occasions and the junctures between them ... It is appropriate to work from the molar level of the plan on down, rather than from the molecular level of the word, gesture, sentence — or even the speech act — on up.

In this way, the organisation of the school year and the class day are important background structures *within* which particular interactional units are placed. The next level of organisation is the formal structure of the school day, although the essential middle-range boundaries of interaction in, say, the elementary school classroom are not *always* provided by the clock or school bell since a 'lesson' can begin before recess and continue after, with little more than a 'bridging' interaction:

T: We'll continue this after recess.
    [... recess]
T: Right. settle down! Now where were we before the bell went?

Thus, the 'lesson' could serve as a suitable middle-range functional unit for many analyses since it defines function and is recognised by participants. However, it must be recognised that several other activities exist at the lesson level: e.g. news sessions; classroom clean-up; snack time; sleep time. This level does not generally demarcate specific linguistic or participant structures, but clusters of them. So we go down one more level. Immediately below the lesson level are a series of lesson segments or sub-occasions, about which participants could say: 'We begin to do something different here or here'. Within a lesson there may be (in order) a teacher monologue, written seat work or group work, a series of teacher questions and pupil answers and a closing teacher monologue. Each of these is defined by different rules for pupil deportment, getting the floor, topic, paying attention and the like. It is at this level that distinctive genres are likely to be found.

Sequences

Our focus in this chapter is on questioning sequences. As stated earlier, the question/answer cycle constitutes the greatest proportion of (official) classroom talk. Many studies have confirmed that teachers ask an average two questions per minute, but averages can be misleading. Actual questioning rates are typically higher than that because significant stretches of lessons have no questions at all. Although most questions in natural speech occur in isolation or small clusters (this is also true of pupil questions), most teacher questions occur in long strings which have a clear unity of purpose. For instance, a teacher might correct the class's answers to last night's homework:

T: OK Who's got question 2 out? ... John?
John: I think the factors are 3 and 12.
T: Right. Anyone have any problems with that one? ... OK Question 3? ... Anyone?

and this will go on until either the questions or time runs out. Or a teacher may be revising earlier work:

T: What role did economic factors play in the lead up to the Civil War? [Pupils put hands up to bid for a chance to answer] Joan?
Joan: I think ... the South got rich so they thought they could do it on their own.
T: How did the South ... what was the basis of their prosperity?

Or introducing/explaining new topics:

T: What do you think about violence in the school? Between kids? ...
C'mon! You must have seen it. How do you feel about it?

Eric: [Calling out] I like to run and join in! [laughter]

T: Go on, Eric. I bet you run the other way. Sensible people would. Come
on! Does it make you scared? I think I can remember back to when I was
your age and it scared me. What do you think?

A sequence of this kind could go on for a long time and contain a cluster of
twenty or thirty teacher questions.

From the analytical point of view it is relatively easy to isolate questioning
sequences from other activities. It is sometimes a little more difficult to detect
shifts of topic or strategy in a long stretch of questioning which can occur with
nothing more than a few intervening words. At the end of a long sequence of
exploratory questions of the kind just illustrated you might get a switch to, say,
revision questions or questions designed to play a different sort of explanatory
role:

T: OK So we all feel scared by violence and sometimes angry. Let's think
back to the poem you studied last night. How does it start? Anyone like to
read the first three lines?

Iteration

A closer look at questioning shows that the strings of questions are made
up of cycles of question/answer/reaction and that the sequences are broken up by
additional elements of interspersed monologues and other moves which function
to summarise or redirect the question sequence. The pattern of such moves tells
us a lot about ownership of problems in the talk. Sinclair and Coulthard[6] code
some of these moves as imbedded Informatives or Directives in and between
sequences of questions (elicitations):

1 Elicit	**T:** Hands up. What can you see, what is the name of the cutter underneath the wood, the name of the cutter underneath the wood?
4 Directive	**T:** You can't tell me because you're not looking at it.
6 Elicit	**T:** The name of the cutter underneath the wood.
7 Answering	**P:** Axe.
8 Follow up	**T:** An axe. Yes, an axe.
9 Directive	**T:** Look at the picture again and put your finger on the scissors.
11 Elicit	**T:** What is the name of the material above the scissors?
13 Answering	**P:** Paper.

14 Follow up **T:** Paper.

....

15 Elicit   **T:** ... Stephen?

....

16 Inform   **T:** Just look. I take metal. [cuts metal] And you can see how it's
cut through.

19 Inform   **T:** Those (edges) are very sharp indeed.

20 Elicit   **T:** Would you like to use these things for cutting things like
paper and cardboard?

22 Answering **P:** [chorus] No![7]

The questions in a sequence are not randomly juxtaposed, as a moment's examination of the above illustrations will show. Question sequences reflect a goal-seeking process or strategy. That is, they raise questions of validity other than those involved in their validity as individual statements. It is only against this strategy, which is often unstated or unannounced, that we can determine the function of individual questions. The interspersed elements, as well as the teacher's reactions to pupil answers, can often provide data on the basis of which we can draw a feasible inference concerning this unstated strategy and the role in it of other elements such as informative moves or directions. The connection between the validity of individual statements and the validity questions raised by their contribution to a wider argument is parallelled by questions of validity concerning the importance of that argument for pupils and teachers. This opens up the connection to questions of motivation and interest again.

A close examination of question/answer cycles and sequences reveals that it is possible to construct a functional typology of question/answer types. The structural predictability of these types permits the application of the concept of genre to them. The blanket category of 'elicit' doesn't capture the difference in the kind of move, functionally and educationally, that we observe between the elicit that admits of a chorus answer (line 20) and that which calls for the pupil to make an inference from evidence (line 11). As Edmondson notes, the category doesn't deal at all well with pupil questions either.[8]

It is important to note here that the genre is not the individual question/answer cycle but the *sequence* of fundamentally similar question/answer cycles within which individual cycles are iterated: e.g. the series of elicits of the name of the material pictured next to each cutting device in the Sinclair and Coulthard example cited above (paper–scissors; metal–hacksaw etc).

Let us begin with a skeleton model and develop it further, introducing both notational conventions and actual rather than skeleton genre elements as we go:

Key: Q = question; A = Answer; R = Teacher Reaction
[Q^A^R]<

The arrow < from *outside* the square brackets means that the cycle Q A R can be repeated or iterated as a whole. The square brackets mean that the sub-structure in the brackets occurs at the location in the sequence where the brackets are found and that all within the square brackets is compulsory. There are no later or earlier sub-structures in this skeleton, but if a whole lesson were to form a genre type it could look like this:

Key: M = Teacher Opening Monologue; C = Teacher Closing Monologue
[M] [Q^A^R]< [C]

where M always occurs before Q A R and C, Q A R (always in that sequence, that's what the ^ means, sometimes but not necessarily iterated <, always after M and before C, and C always after Q A R (and M of course).

Obligatory and Optional Elements of Genres

Classroom questioning genres are a little different from some other genres because the genre structure is short and reiterated. In addition, and somewhat paradoxically, some elements can be compulsory but not show up in all situations because, as Mehan has shown, they are 'understood' in all due to their presence in many.[9]

So a modification to the way the genre concept is usually applied in analysis is necessary. Obligatory elements need not always be present to affect all of the genre. The different functions of the question form mean that gross form is not a good guide to function. Generic differences are indicated by subtle lexico-grammatical and phonological cues. The same surface form (e.g. question, statement, exclamation, etc.) doesn't constitute the same function and it is functionally differing elements that distinguish one genre from another — necessary sequences of functional elements. This is a corollary of the fact that the same surface forms may function in many different ways, always functional several ways at once, and the converse, that the same functions may be realised by many forms.

Functionally different strategies

Now let us differentiate Q A R (sounds like the calculus, doesn't it?). What sort of questioning strategies do teachers pursue? And how may different kinds of questions occur in them? What follows is an attempt to identify some of these, but it is not necessarily exhaustive of all possible genres, since it relates to a statistically small corpus of only 70 lessons. In addition, the level of the analysis means that it must be accorded only a provisional status.

A few common-sense possibilities have already been suggested — checking answers to written questions, revising old work, introducing new topics — but I would like to take a more analytic approach. The contextual configuration (the values of field, tenor and mode) is what guides the structuring of an interactional text. It would be appropriate to begin by defining the variety of classroom tasks, relationships, agent roles and linguistic expectations, styles and so on that differing questioning strategies might employ, and to use these predictively to locate regular textual differences. This will then be applied to the Q/A cycle.

In doing this we will probe below the surface level of teacher question/pupil answer/teacher's evaluation of pupil answer/teacher's comment on student answer, which is common to questioning sequences of very different functional kinds, to try to locate different kinds of questions, answers, evaluation and comments. Behavioural research has established that the general structural 'shape' of most questioning exchanges is similar. The 'cycle' begins with a teacher question, followed by a pupil answer, then a teacher reaction to the pupil answer. This has been called Initiate–Respond–Feedback (IRF) and Question–Answer–Reaction (QAR). What I am seeking to establish is that within this very general structure there are several functionally quite different (and therefore educationally quite different) genres of teacher questioning; each of these genres will have a different *configuration* of the values of field/tenor/mode. The stress on 'configuration' here permits some values to be the same. In both the 'shopping' and the 'bargaining' genres the field was characterised by the buyer seeking to make a purchase and the seller a sale, etc.; however, other aspects of field were different: the buyer was seeking to purchase what was wanted *at the lowest possible price*, and so on. That bargaining is a different genre and not merely the same genre with a different pattern of optional elements is indicated by a *qualitative* difference in moves which are otherwise similar on the surface, and, possibly by the compulsory nature of elements in the bargaining game which were only 'optional' in the shopping genre. Each questioning genre must be distinguished in the same way.

Let us first look at the general background elements (or variables) of field and tenor, before distinguishing the different values that may be taken on by them in particular genres. First, I will remind you of the dominant cultural context and then counter-cultural views. Observational and ethnographic research generally shows our schools to be 'conservative'; in them, pupils learn a curriculum which is to a greater or lesser degree set by school boards or school district administrators and interpreted by schools and teachers. Although different parts of the curriculum admit of some degree of choice and diversity in practice, teachers' actual interpretations of choice often reproduce a convergence. By and large, classroom learning is about pupils learning what teachers tell them to learn, and teachers do not have (or exercise) a great deal of choice about what they tell students to learn.

The general task definition of classroom teaching is that pupils will learn the set curriculum. This is the general task of the classroom: to 'cover' (i.e. get through) the set curriculum and for pupils to achieve a reasonable level of 'mastery' of it while teachers have sufficient control to do all this (Smith and Geoffrey).

The agent roles are teacher and learner (pupil). The teacher's task is to bring about learning: this is called teaching. It is generally seen to be a directive, active thing to do. The learning to be done is covered on a week by week, semester by semester basis at a more or less planned rate. New material is introduced, worked with, revised and tested, then more new material is introduced, worked with and so on. From time to time material covered over a series of such cycles is revised and tested — for instance, at the end of a semester or year. The material to be learned is divided into 'topics'. At a later stage, topics may be built on, related to others, or combined.

Questioning, insofar as it requires answering, can play a number of roles in this process. It can 'motivate' learners, for instance, by interesting them. It can be used to revise. It can be used to test or assess. It can be used to control. It can be used to explore, explain or explicate. A question which seeks to assess a pupil's knowledge (by seeing if the answer matches the teacher's view of the correct answer) may have a similar surface form to a question which seeks to interest a student, or find out something a teacher *doesn't* know, but it is fundamentally different *educationally*.

If there is a general dimension to the function of questioning (at least questions that seek answers) it is this: to find out what another person knows, thinks or feels. Where the clearest differences may emerge is in the purpose or goal of such finding out — that will determine the strategy; the *line* of questioning. It is important to remember that we are concerned with a group of genres that are typically iterated — with questioning rather than isolated questions. Of course, questioning can be carried out with no interest in finding out. There can be a series of rhetorical questions (but then there will be no answers or the questioners will answer their own questions), or a questioning that is merely conventional or polite and where the answers are a ritual response that carry no new information. In such a case, there is little or no real 'finding out':

B: Good morning, John
J: Good morning, Bill. How are you?
B: Fine. How are *you*?
J: Fine. How's the family?
B: Oh! They're fine.

Logically, we can ring the changes on the subject matter of the question in a number of ways. This is a good starting point because the general function of questions is to find out or gain knowledge of some kind. The question can be about something the questioner does or does not know; the answerer may or may not be expected to know the answer. In an educational context, knowing or not knowing the answer you might be expected to know can be of crucial significance. (See Figure 1: The category designations in the boxes are produced from the answerer's point of view)

The kind of 'telling' that would be likely to occur in Box 2 in the conventional classroom would probably be about extra-curricular knowledge, such as pupil's background, whether they have done their homework, etc. By and large pupils are not expected to make significant subject matter contribution which the teacher cannot also make.

Further elements of context may be introduced to differentiate within some of the cells in this model. When a teacher asks for some information he or she

QUESTIONER

		Already knows answer	Doesn't already know
A	answerer	1. Being tested	2. Telling the
N	expected to	or	questioner
S	know	assessed	what she wants to
W			know
E			
R	Answerer	3. Being 'Socratized'	4. Start of
E	not expected	or asked to guess	shared inquiry
R	to know	or infer	

FIGURE 1 *Teachers' questions*

already possesses it is in some sense an assessment. But the purpose of such assessment could be to find out what the pupil's prior knowledge is in order not to waste time by teaching what is already known (diagnostic questioning), or it could be to evaluate and grade the student's performance (competitive testing). Similarly, shared inquiry will not emerge from an unanswered question unless the question becomes *owned* by the answerer as well as the original questioner. Again, simple finding out is not so simple. These are differences at the level of *questioning* (rather than single questions) between, say, finding out in order to evaluate in some way, and finding out in order to satisfy curiosity or resolve a misunderstanding.

Now take the locus of authority — the agent role which governs official control over conduct and correctness of *content*. In the conventional classroom this virtually identifies 'questioner' with 'teacher'. As classroom observation shows, pupils typically ask as few as ten questions each *per annum*; teachers may ask 10,000 in a year. Hugh Mehan has observed that teachers evaluate virtually all pupil answers but pupils do not (overtly) evaluate teacher answers. This is just the opposite of what you would expect if learners were making their own validity judgements as part of a public process of shared inquiry. In the typical classroom revealed by most observational research, teachers initiate questioning sequences, control their strategy or direction, control topic by either sustaining it or changing it by fiat, and remain virtually sole arbiters of correct answers. The logically possible alternative of Box 4 is found in only a small percentage of classrooms.

The descriptions in the boxes in Figure 2 are from the teacher's viewpoint this time. The pupil's agent role is obviously quite different from that of the teacher, and pupil discourse has a different status and function from teacher's discourse. In the conventional classroom, the teacher is expected to know the subject matter. When pupils ask questions about the subject matter that the teacher cannot answer it is often treated as an embarrassment, particularly if the subject matter is one in which the teacher is regarded as expert (e.g. the chemistry teacher on a chemistry question). Box 4 of pupil questions is thus anomalous or marginal in terms of the agent role relationship of the conventional classroom. Perhaps that is why, according to observers, many such questions are not answered. Conversely, Box 2, as mentioned, is likely to be confined to pupils asking about non-subject matter knowledge, often of a procedural or personal kind. (We would expect this kind of question from teachers in, say, a motivational strategy or a social/control exchange.)

Of course, not all classrooms are like this. But, as much as those of us who are teachers would deny the description, the observational data should give us pause. Most pupil questions are about matters of routine: 'How wide should we

QUESTIONER (Pupil)

		Knows	Does not know
[			
[	Answerer	1. Pupil	2. Pupil
[	expected	showing	finding
[	to know	off?	something
[			out.
ANSWERER [			
(Teacher) [	Answerer	3. Smart	4. 'Come and
[	may not	ass!	see me at recess.'
[	know		
[			

FIGURE 2 *Pupils' questions*

rule the margin? Which questions should we do?' Those questions which are about the subject matter (one in ten) are as often as not fobbed off with remarks like: 'That's an interesting issue but we haven't time for it now. Come and see me later.'

On the basis of the foregoing analysis of the conventional classroom, we might expect that however many genres of teacher questions there are, these will be able to be grouped into four broad functional groupings on the basis of the knowledge/ignorance distribution. But within these categories we might expect significant functional differences depending on the definitions of the agent roles and the task/strategy. The distinction between diagnostic testing and competitive testing has already been mentioned. Whether this would express itself in essential differences of structure or reflect only differences in the distribution of optional elements remains to be seen. The same might be said for 'being Socratized'. A humanistic or evocative questioning sequence might be an invitation for conformity to the teacher's pre-decided right answer in the well-known game of 'Guess what teacher thinks' rather than a provocation to the exploration of a question. The difference might well be in successive evaluations/comments: if they are in the order of 'Getting warm ... No! Getting cold', then we have probably got a (GWTT) (Guess What Teacher Thinks). But what is the alternative to this, if the teacher already 'knows the answer'? Perhaps it is a methodological strategy, in which the teacher abstains from a focus on 'the right answer' but uses his or her knowledge of the subject matter to help in formulating questions which guide the *methodology* of the pupil's thinking towards an answer which is not just a guess but based on reasoning and evidence.

Finally, Box 4 (Figure 1), of course, may be simulated, as it sometimes is in 'neutral chairperson' teaching. This is not necessarily a 'bad thing' educationally, but it is difficult to maintain a strictly non-directive role when you (a) have the cognitive authority and (b) know the answer. This general group of questioning strategies is quite rare in either the literature of observation or the corpus of transcripts available to the author. For obvious reasons, it is of theoretical interest because it approximates the notion of 'conversational action' discussed in Chapter 3.

The four hypothetical groups of genres in Figure 1 could be subdivided into two clusters, a 'method' classroom cluster and a 'discourse' classroom cluster. The method cluster consists of Boxes 1, 2 and 3. The remaining box is the discourse. What the method classrooms share in common is a definition of the *general task* of the classroom, of which the *task of questioning* is a sub-task. The method classroom is about teaching a set curriculum and about preserving the knowledge selected for that curriculum like a fly in the amber of decontextualisation. The discourse classroom is about helping the pupil to 'grow up' *into* the discourse of the species, in all its variety and uncertainty and change.

The *agent roles* of the teacher and pupil vary along the same lines. In the *method* classroom, the teacher, as Barnes has said, is a transmitter of knowledge: the teacher 'teaches'. In the *discourse* classroom, the teacher interprets and fosters inquiry. In the former, the teacher is the expert and the knowledge already fixed. The issue is to transmit it and check whether it has stuck or not, by getting the pupil to repeat it back. The teacher is *the* authority since she *already knows*. In the discourse classroom, the teacher's adult expertise is tempered by the knowledge that the purpose is not simply to transmit a set curriculum, although there may be areas of knowledge which are considered important, but to foster the pupil's participation in inquiry. The teacher is *in* authority, since she is closer to being a fully fledged participant in the discourse than the pupil and usually, in a school setting, has responsibility for regulating the conduct of a group of inquirers, but she has the authority that a guide or pilot has relative to the captain of a ship, rather than the combined authority of both captain *and* pilot relative to the passengers.

Within the two broad clusters of agent roles and task definitions there may be found a variety of questioning genres and groups of genres. In the next chapter we will deal with examples of both — the dominant patterns found in our schools (Figure 1: Boxes 1, 2 and 3) and alternatives (Box 4).

Some Features of Questioning Genres of the Method Classroom

	Teacher	Pupil
From Box 1: Reproduction Questioning (What Do Pupils Know)		
Field (task)	to discover if the pupils 'know' what was taught	to give back what has been taught
Tenor		
Agent Roles:	(i) to ask a series of questions in such a way as to cover the subject matter	(i) to bid for a chance to answer when told
	(ii) to let pupils know whether their answers are correct	(ii) to answer in *the way* the teacher wants
	(iii) to correct pupil errors	(iii) to correct errors pointed out by the teacher
Social Distance:	[As usual in the classroom it is High to Maximal]	
Mode		
Language Role:	[Constitutive and canonical]	
Process Sharing:	[Yes]	
Channel:	[Phonic spoken with visual contact]	
From Box 2: Inductive Questioning (Guess What Teacher Thinks)		
Field	to get students to identify their prior knowledge and to motivate them to further inquiry	to try to think what the teacher is getting at and to join in
Tenor		
Agent Roles:	(i) to pursue a strategy which will draw out student knowledge, leading them to inductive conclusions	(i) to guess what teacher thinks. To guess or infer
	(ii) to let pupils know if their guesses are getting warmer or cooler	(ii) to be sensitive to clues. To take up the teacher's viewpoint

(Continued)

	Teacher	*Pupil*
	(iii) to reach a satisfactory conclusion	(iii) to reach the conclusion before the teacher has to tell everyone what it is

Social Distance:	[Less than for Box 1 but still fairly high]
Mode	
Language Role:	[Constitutive but with the boundary between canonical and personal language blurred. Answers may be stated first in personal language without penalty provided they can subsequently be put into canonical language]
Process Sharing:	[Yes]
Channel:	[Phonic spoken with visual contact]

From Box 3: Finding Out

Field	The teacher needs to know something about the pupil for administrative reasons. This is usually an item of everyday rather than curriculum knowledge	The pupil must provide the information (unless too personal)
Tenor		
Agent Roles:	The teacher is asking pursuant to classroom management or possibly establishing something straightforward about pupil's background learning	The pupils answer clearly and honestly

Social Distance:	[Variable but not low]
Mode	
Language Role:	[Constitutive]
Process Sharing:	[Yes]
Channel	[Phonic spoken with visual contact]

Now let us examine some textual examples of these and contrast them with the contextual configuration and some textual examples of Figure 1, Box 4.

8 Critical Discourse in Classrooms

Examples of Questioning Genres

The texts presented for analysis here have been selected from the corpus for their illustrative value, but almost any random selection would have displayed much the same set of features. The purpose of the analysis is to display the constraints identified in the structural analysis of Chapter 6 and to show how it is possible to teach in a way which constrains pupil talk less. Only two transcripts in the corpus displayed patterns related to Box 4. The analysis is pursued only as far as is necessary to make the points made, but readers may take it further if they wish. Examples of What Do Pupils Know (WDPK) and Guess What Teacher Thinks (GWTT) are dealt with first, then Discursive teaching is illustrated (D).

WDPK 1

T: Now the first thing I want to ask you is what's the meaning of this term [points to chalkboard] ... divine right. Lyn?

P: It's a belief that the king got his right to rule straight from God and to answer to God only, and nobody else.

T: Good. Very good! Now what I've got here are a couple of illustrations that go a little bit further on this idea of divine right because we all know Charles the First firmly believed in his divine right.

P: If Charles wanted money and parliament wouldn't give it.

T: Fine. And this amounted to conflict — what is another word for conflict — we say that the parliament what against the king?

P: Grievances against the king.

T: Grievances. Very good!

Here, I am working from a transcript I didn't collect myself. I am limited to the thinner communicative evidence of the transcript rather than to the thicker data of an audio tape or, even better, a video tape. It is fairly clear from internal evidence that this material has been previously introduced and is now being revised and perhaps extended. The word 'grievances' has a clear smack of previously introduced terminology about it. 'We all know' also signals this. The lesson goes on to explore the area of conflict between king and parliament more deeply than it had been in the previous lesson. Some WDPK questions occur in this reminding/checking role as single questions or sequences of two or three, where a teacher wants to check a point from previous work because he or she is about to build on that. At other times, when the teacher is 'doing' revision, they may occur in long sequences. Strictly speaking what we have here appears to be a cousin of WDPK, since the purpose appears to be as much to remind the pupils of what they already know prior to going on. as to ascertain their knowledge for the teacher's assessment or diagnostic purposes.

You can see here the teacher question/pupil answer/teacher evaluation ('fine', 'good')/rest of teacher reaction structure clearly, although in the final cycle the evaluation comes after the rest of the reaction (which is probably a repetition with intonation of approval).

WDPK 2

> (Note: .... means section omitted)
> (... within a line of dialogue means a pause)
> **T:** [Draws triangle on chalkboard] Stephen?
> **P:** [Stephen goes to board and draws in axis of symmetry]
> **T:** Anyone like to say anything about that one?
> ....
> Does it have *another* axis of symmetry? ... Michelle?
> **M:** Yes.
> **T:** Michelle, I don't think so.
> ... [indicating line Stephen has drawn] Do you think Stephen's line is correct?
> **M:** Yes.
> **T:** Why?
> **M:** Because if you fold it in half they will be exact.
> **T:** What sort of triangle is it, Mark?
> **P:** Isosceles.
> **T:** Isosceles. [draws second triangle on board] ... Kay?
> **P:** [Kay comes to board and draws in axis of symmetry] ... Everyone agree?
> .... [and so on for many repetitions] ....

This is a little closer to WDPK. The questioning here serves a dual purpose: it is drilling correct use of the concept of symmetry while also checking that each pupil in the class can apply it. The teacher evaluation of the reply 'isosceles' is phonological not lexical — (repetition with intonation of approval).

In the WDPK genre the pupils seem to know that their role is to show that they can reproduce what has been taught. These examples are from classrooms that seem 'normal' enough. The second example might even be regarded as an example of reasonably competent teaching. Why, then, are these examples being considered here as a fit subject for criticism? The answer must be that in a given classroom they may not be a fit subject for criticism. Criticism in the abstract is dangerous because it doesn't and cannot take circumstances into account. Much teaching will be like this teaching. Only *in* a situation and in the light of some degree of curricular freedom can a criticism be sustained. The questions for *critique*, then, are whether or not there are more educative alternatives to this pattern and whether or not there are situations in which these alternatives might feasibly be used.

A clear alternative would be provided by a talk structure through which a pupil or pupils took *responsibility* for rehearsing what they knew, in the same way as someone seeking to investigate a problem or make an important decision might take a piece of paper and make a list of 'things known' and 'questions to answer'. Again, responsibility for correcting such lists can be taken by pupils. An individual or group, given time, and spurred on by shrewd questions, can often identify the presence of errors, omissions and contradictions in their own recently given account and attempt to reason their way through to a correction that will be associated with a lasting and systematic improvement in their understanding of a subject, as well as in their self-confidence as learners.

Now the point of this should be clear. It is *not* that teachers should adopt different communication structures in classrooms when they want to check pupils' knowledge or to revise a topic. There may not be sufficient time for that, or there may be other problems in a given situation. The point *is* that they should recognise that alternative structures do exist, and that they should critically evaluate the structures they are using and the alternatives in terms of their educational value and introduce alternatives where it is valuable *and* feasible to do so.

GWTT 1

T: Why do people have discussions?
        ....
P: To get each other's opinions.
T: Good. To get each other's opinions ...
P: [inaudible ...]
T: All right, and to find out what each other thinks about things and perhaps come to an [rising intonation] ... [pause with raised eyebrows] ...
P: Agreement.

T: ... [pause] decision about something. Alright, you might have a problem, you discuss it with someone. They might help you to solve it.

T: When ... when in your life have you been involved in a discussion?

....

P: When the deputy principal interviews you.

All: [Laughter]

T: Well I don't know that that's actually a discussion.

P: Handball ... when it's on the line and everyone disagrees with you.

T: Come on! Think! Other situations at school.

P: In the playground?

T: Good. In the playground ... [here follows several questions and answers about school]

T: ... Let's just forget about school for a moment.

P: [Putting hand up]

T: Yes? [pupil shakes head]

T: [To whole class again] At home. When could your family be involved in a discussion?

....

T: Now what is a discussion about? ... someone having an idea. You might disagree with it and you throw your ideas back and forth.

[P: That's really an argument.

[P: That's an argument!

[P: Argument.

P: I think that's a debate, really.

T: Well, a debate is a more formal discussion, isn't it? I'm sort of thinking of things informally at home ...

P: That's an argument. When you're fighting back.

T: No, it doesn't have to be an argument ... Can you think of situations where you might be involved in a discussion ... Either the debate kind that John talked about or the argument kind that Joan talked about? I'm going to classify all those as discussions.

This is a clear example of GWTT. The game is what the teacher thinks. It is she who declares the meaning of a discussion in a break for a small monologue in the questioning sequence (... you might have a problem. You discuss it with someone, etc.). Her definitions are the object of the command 'Think!'(*I'm* going to classify ...). She clearly controls topic (Let's just forget about school ...). When she says 'Well I don't know that that's actually a discussion', she is announcing that the game is to guess what she does know. The clues for this game of twenty questions are contained in several small definitional monologues like the one illustrated and in several legislative moves of the kind which begins 'I'm going to classify'. At several points in the very long game (180 lines of typescript), she speaks of what she knows or means, although it is more often expressed as 'What do *we* mean by ...'[1] Here is an example of both:

T: ... Now when in your life have you been involved in a discussion?
P: Never.
P: When my mum gets on the phone for six hours with Auntie Barbara and I ask her when's tea [general laughter].
T: ... So you can have discussions at home, but that, I don't know that that's actually a discussion. That's one question and you get an answer. What do *we* really mean when *we* talk about a discussion? Do *we* mean just one question and one answer?
[emphasis added]

The inclusive plural is also used in GWTT sequences where the subject matter of the lesson contains less debatable views:

(In a science lesson where a small foil propellor is placed over a flame and is spun by the rising air)
T: But what happens to the air?
P: It gets warm.
T: Yes, it gets warm and what happens to it then?
P: It rises.
T: So what happens?
ALL: Hot air rises!
T: Right. So *our* conclusion is that hot air rises.
[emphasis added][2]

Normally when a teacher ignores a pupil answer and recycles the question it indicates that the answer is wrong.[3] The pupil who answered 'It rises' was obviously correct, but the form was not canonical. When the question was recycled the whole class correctly intuited that the error was one of form, not substance. The teacher was then able to announce the conclusion as theirs. This is an instance of a general feature of the dominant pattern of classroom communication:

The teacher provides the framework into which pupil talk is fitted, and that talk is assessed according to the closeness of fit. Brief pupil contributions are taken as being representative of the group, and the interaction then proceeds *as though* the other pupils either knew or already shared the same and now *corrected* inadequacies as those who spoke ... the interaction can be seen as the managed product of one of its participants.[4]

The validity that is at stake is not validity in the rational sense. It is validity in a distorted sense. The pupil is not expected to make an independent validity judgement on the basis of his or her own experience, but to accept the teacher's. Validity is judged by the teacher, on the basis of the closeness of fit of pupil answers to what the teacher thinks. This is a process in which the teacher as *an* authority on the subject matter is converted into being *in* authority not just over the conduct of the work of the classroom but over the subject matter. There is no educational justification for this kind of questioning, and it is difficult to imagine that any given set of curricular constraints could require it rather than a more educational alternative. Despite this, the pattern is very common in the introduction of new work and in the development stages of a topic.

GWTT 2

T: What is the reason for people writing things down?

P: So that they can give you the knowledge they have so that you can learn it.

T: They want to give you the information so that you can learn it. Sometimes it's only for enjoyment but they want you to find out something. Is that right? There's a big word that means that ... quite a long word ... Not 'a hard on', John ... I'll give you a clue what it is. It begins with a 'c' and it gives you the aims that this person has all the time when writing ... I'll give you another clue, another letter, 'o'.

P: Composition?

T: Very nearly ... not quite right ... no.

P: Comprehension?

T: Well, it is comprehension ... that's quite true ... it is comprehension because you are going to understand what the person is saying but this person is trying to carry out a method of [rising intonation] ...

P: Communicate.

T: Good boy! Can you make it into a noun for me ... it's a verb, 'communicate' ... You call it communication.

P: Communication.

T: Good boy! Communication. And that's the whole purpose of writing ... to try to communicate with people.

This example is of a kind found quite frequently imbedded in other types of questioning sequence. The terminology guessing game is replete with clue-giving that is sometimes actually called clue-giving as opposed to the small definitional monologue in the previous example.[5] Here is another example:

T: ... What did she add? What's the name of it?

P: Strength?

T: ... The word I am thinking of starts with an 'e' ...

P: Exasperation?

T: I don't think so. Exasperation is when you're annoyed ... [...] ... She didn't just read the words, she made them much more meaningful, because she added this dimension and it starts with 'e', the word I'm thinking about.[6]

Exasperated? I'm not going to tell you what teacher thinks. *You* guess!

The full specification of the GSP for each of these is beyond the scope of the present very exploratory argument. It is sufficient for the present purpose to make the case that in each of these categories, if not in each example, the teacher's questions constitute a functionally different kind of move. Taken with the whole set of contextual assumptions and related interpretive strategies which pupils bring to answering, a strong case can be made out that the question 'What is another word for conflict?' could not admit of 'strife', 'fighting', 'discord' or 'contention' as acceptable answers, because the question, in its full paralinguistic and extralinguistic[7] context, was one which was asking for reproduction of previously given information in standard terminology. One of the limitations of a transcript is that there is sometimes no specific lexical cue to a functional difference. The markers can be phonological. The pupil responses in GWTT are often marked by a rising intonation, indicated in the example immediately above by question marks — 'Exasperation?'. What you cannot see from the transcript of GWTT 1 above is that the video tape shows raised eyebrows and the audio track frequent questioning intonations. Similarly, the flatter intonation, with, at times, almost quiz-masterish overtones (Right. We'll see if you can do *this* one!) of the questions in WDPK doesn't show up in the transcript. An appropriate name for this element of the GSP would be *'reproduction question'*, and within that category, the sub-category 'terminological', to distinguish it from the standard reproduction question 'Why did Charles fight with the parliament?' which calls for the reasons given in a previous lesson to be reproduced.

The questions in WDPK 2, 'Does it have another axis of symmetry?' and 'What sort of triangle is it, Mark?' seem at first to be a little different. But when the teacher draws an isosceles triangle and asks what sort it is (when the class has already 'done' isosceles triangles), we have a question very similar to the situation where a teacher writes the words 'divine right' on the board and asks '... what's the meaning of this term?' where that has already been given. Such questions readily shade into questions where pupils have to make new connections or display skills in non-routine ways. When axis of symmetry was first being introduced (in a previous lesson), and the vertical axis of symmetry on an equilateral triangle was shown on an example, the question 'Does it have another axis of symmetry?' would call for an insight which generalised the vertical case to all three sides of the triangle — an educationally and functionally different question. A delicate analysis of the phonology of a question like that would probably give indications of the teacher signalling 'OK now, here's a hard one!', if, in fact, verbal markers were not also present.[8]

The type of question which characterises GWTT might be called '*guessing invitation*' question. The 'guess what word I'm thinking of' version could be called the terminological sub-category. Again, the markers of this kind of question are not necessarily in the lexical form. There are, for instance, intonational differences in evaluations, reminiscent of guessing games. In reproduction questions the 'no' indicating a wrong answer is usually fairly flat. In guessing games it takes on a characteristic coy warble, with a fall then a rise in the course of the word — 'No ... u'. The contrast between all other teaching examples and the matter-of-factness of teacher questions and pupil answers when the questions are simple Finding Out (FO) is marked. But examples of this are rare:

T: Did you give that note to Mr Barker, John?
P: Yes, sir.
T: When did you give it to him? Before lunch?

The points made above are mostly not new. Many critically sensitive teachers have been aware of these issues for some time. Even from the standpoint of teaching the set curriculum, these questioning strategies are not efficient. The GWTT type seldom generates real thinking. As often as not, teachers give so many clues that they come close to answering their own questions. Sometimes they go even further, as Ira Shor points out: 'Do you know what many teachers do when facing student silence or one syllable answers? Teachers start answering their own questions!'[9] They also do much of the higher order cognitive work in classrooms. When a student answer is defective (in other than the sense of being in non-canonical form) the answer is repeated with changes or paraphrased, but changed, so that it emerges as correct but still purporting to be a representation of pupil speech. This formulating practice, or reformulating practice, is usually carried out without explicit reference to the nature of the defect in the pupil's original utterance:

T: What's inflation?
P: Well, I'd say the rising prices.
T: The *general* rising prices of products ...
[emphasis added][10]

The cognitive work is simply *done*. One assumes the defective answer is analysed in some way, although often the only evidence for that lies in hesitancy phenomena in teacher speech[11] as the teacher pauses to reorganise and re-express the pupil's speech:

(from GWTT 1)

P: Agreement.

T: ... [pause] *decision* about something.

The pupil's incorrect, or at least imperfect, answer is formulated as a canonically correct answer without *either* an acknowledgement that a correction has been made *or* an expression of the reason for the correction. The former process is common enough in ordinary speech. Jefferson speaks of 'embedded corrections': these have the characteristic that they do not make the process of correction the topical focus of the talk, and so interrupt the business of the talk. The alternative form of correction in ordinary talk is 'exposed correction' in which the topic of the talk is suspended for a moment while there is a brief focusing on a correction.[12] Here we can see a germ of an explanation of why teachers seem to prefer embedded correction. It does not require an 'interruption' to the focus on the content of the lesson.

However, the results of this preference seem educationally dubious. If we define making mistakes, recognising we have made them, understanding why they are mistakes and correcting them as an important part of learning, then what is happening in the process identified is that the teachers are doing this rather than the pupils. When we add in the elements of context present but not obvious in the transcript, such as pre-existing frameworks of validity commitments and some context in which an action was taken which did not succeed (followed by recognition of error, understanding it, correcting it etc.), we can see that what is at stake here is problem solving learning itself. This teacher's approach to questioning not only robs the pupil of the opportunity to respond to the truth/validity claims being made, by reserving this kind of response for the teacher (as expressed in teacher evaluations and formulations of pupil answers), it finishes up *by requiring the teacher to do the learning instead of the pupil!*

Note that in the discussion of inflation above, the teacher's answer is also wrong, in the teacher's own terms, since inflation is the rise in the prices of all traded 'goods', including services as well as products; but the teacher was so intent on generalising the pupil's answer, he lost sight of this. An alternative strategy would have been to ask:

T: OK. The rising prices. That's fine as far as it goes, but tell me what prices
we are talking about here.

In this way, if the issue of generality is important, it can be made briefly topical, and the pupil can correct her own thinking. While this would not necessarily mean that the pupil's own problematic was engaged, it would at least give the pupil the opportunity to reason. Again, the point is not to say teachers must do this or that, but to identify alternative possibilities and draw out their educational implications. Let us look at an actual example of an alternative genre in action followed by two textual examples.

	Teacher	Pupil
From Box 4: Discursive (D)		
Field	The teacher seeks to engage the pupil in the discourse	The pupil tries to make sense of the subject
Tenor		
Agent Roles:	The teacher is responsible for scaffolding and quality control and sharing the inquiry	The pupil is responsible for her own learning
Social Distance:	[Relatively low]	
Mode		
Language Role:	[Constitutive but personal, moving into canonical as conclusions reached]	
Process Sharing:	[Yes, in a high degree]	
Channel:	[As usual]	

D 1

T: But that television tape you saw said that violence on television didn't have much effect on people.

P: But that was just a theory.

T: You really think that it does have some effect?

P: [nods]

T: OK.

....

P: I think it's probably a lot easier for you to take er the violent way out of solving their differences rather than to be more diplomatic.

[**T:** That would relate then with ...

[**P:** Yes.

[**T:** ... Eric's view that it's an issue of self-control?

....

T: So the vandals who destroy railway trains are people who haven't got friends to fight with. Don't they get their friends to help them unscrew the seats?

[**P:**   Aw, I suppose … [starting to retract view expressed]
[**T:**   I … no, no, I'm just getting you to test out your generalisation … Think it
         out and if you still think it …

....

T: Well then, let me test out your assumption that adults tend to act differently.
         Do you think that *all* adults act this way? What about … etc.

....

T: It seems to me that you're bringing two ideas together that don't belong …
         Now is it because they don't have any sport to play or is it because they are
         bored?

....

T: We are both generalising about a situation we don't know a great deal about
         and that's always difficult.

....

T: Do you think Billy [a fictional character] was afraid of being hurt in the
         fight? … Would being afraid of being hurt have stopped Billy, do you
         think?
P: No, he was begging … sort of, he's had to fight and then started pegging
         back stones, so
T: Yes, he was almost looking for it.
P: I reckon that's wrong, because he was crying.
[**T:**   Yes, he was crying but then …
[**P:**   I think it was …
T: Oh, what's your comment on that before I make one?
P: I think it could have been tears of rage.
T: Yeah, I think so. Don't you … well, I can't remember when I last had a
         fight … [general laughter] … when you're in a fight don't you get to the
         stage when you want to … sort of feel like the tears of frustration pouring
         down your face?
P: It could be like that, but also he, sort of, he thinks he's been defeated, so
         he's crying …
T: Yes, he possibly does. I think possibly both things come into it. John?
P: On the other hand, he only starts crying when Mr. Farthing comes up and …
T: … gives support to him. Yes, he starts straight away crying and gets some
         support, somebody shows him a bit of sympathy so he …
P: … caves in.
T: Caves in somewhat.

This text displays a number of rare features. First, the evaluations: there is
an evaluation function here of simple acceptance of someone's view as their
view and as *prima facie* a legitimate view, not as 'Good!' or bad according to
the teacher's version of the truth. If this teacher feels a view is problematic, the

reasons for its being seen that way are made topical — e.g. overgeneralisation, generalisation on a thin data base — rather than the more common pattern in the method classroom of simply saying 'no'. In this way, the teacher responds to something seen as problematic to him or her with questions or with counter-claims, that is, in the speech role of a fellow inquirer. The pupils then have to make good their own claims with reason and evidence. Their claims are responded to as arguments to be taken seriously, but they are not simply allowed to 'do their own thing'. Their claims are claims *on* the teacher and the other students, who can and should check their validity. Because of this, the question of 'standards' cannot validly be raised by opponents of critical teaching. The students themselves, with the teacher, as a group, become responsible for standards. The teacher doesn't magisterially do it all for them. Their rights and responsibilities as members of the problem-posing, knowing and deciding community are 'in the picture' rather than their answering behaviour, considered solely in terms of closeness of fit to a pre-given model. The ownership of the view and the responsibility for fixing any problems in it, *or* successfully meeting and overcoming the teacher's challenge to it, remains with the pupil. The teacher 'keeps track' of view ownership, as do the pupils at various points in the lesson, by the use of ownership markers[13] — 'As John said', 'That would relate with Eric's view that ...'. The pupils evidently take this seriously because they do contradict the teacher, qualify points he has made, and add to them:

T: Gerry?
P: I had a personal experience at my old school in third class, I think [general laughter] er, a long time ago, but see these blokes were picking on me and I wouldn't fight.
T: Mmm.
P: ... from then on they were really good friends of mine.
T: So you'd what ...?
[**P:** Thinking of me as a buddy ...
[**T:** So you, you'd destroy my case in flames at one hit. Ah, that's fine though. I think that's important.

The conclusion reached above about Billy is a product not simply of the kind of linguistic collaboration that is necessary for lessons to happen at all,[14] but collaboration at the level of *analysis* of the text they are studying — collaboration in the reasoning of the subject matter, in the discourse of the subject. The agent roles of this form of collaboration are roles of joint rational responsibility, although the teacher's role remains one of 'leadership' in the sense of taking a special, continuing and methodological responsibility (in the sense that the teacher takes responsibility for critique of the quality of pupil reasoning). In the traditional method classroom, the teacher's methodological responsibility is discharged tacitly, by the teacher's application of tacit critique to pupil answers, rather than topically, by overt critique and claim or counter-claim. In the structure illustrated here, the teacher avoids the constraints on bad teaching discussed at the end of Chapter 6. The teacher takes on a responsibility for the development of reasoning *in the talk* by asking clarifying questions (So you'd what ...?) and by careful paraphrase, accompanied by another rare talk move, the use of confirmation/disconfirmation invitations:

P: Well, Sir, they um might not have the verbal ... er ... power to express what they want to so they just hit out.

T: Lacking, alright, you're suggesting that perhaps where you haven't got the verbal skills, is that what you're suggesting?

P: Yes.

T: [To another P who evidently doesn't like this answer much] Would you agree with that?

Confirmation/disconfirmation invitations following paraphrases are rare, but in this classroom there are many. Rarer still are they taken seriously and answered in the positive. Still rarer are those answered in the negative, but this lesson contains one. There is still talk asymmetry in this classroom, but it is a different asymmetry from that in the dominant classroom type. This asymmetry is complementary, since the rights of pupils as rational interlocutors are preserved, while the teacher's superior knowledge and rational skills are still able to be employed on the pupils' behalf in the fostering of the inquiry of the class. Complementary asymmetry of this kind is educational teaching. It is what justifies the presence of a teacher. The talk functions specific to the teacher in these structures are what defines their agent role *as* either educative teacher or mere instructor.

In another text, a teacher adds another ingredient — a structuring of the talk so that pupils ask the questions:

D 2

(In a class discussion on migration and ethnic prejudice)

T: ... Any of your parents migrate?

P: A long time ago.

T: Fairly recently? ... I suppose then that I'm the only recent migrant. I came out with a plane load of other migrants. We arrived at Mascot early one morning ... went into a line at immigration ... Behind the desk is the Immigration Department Officer. His job is to interview you. Each one of you is that official and I'm standing here in front of your desk. What questions do you ask me?

P: Why did you come out to Australia?

T: Why?

P: When are you going? (general laughter)
T: Fair go mate! [An Australian expression — general laughter]
P: Have you got any employment?
T: Please?

....

T: Mr Lynch, who was then minister of immigration said, 'We don't want a divided society'. What do you think he meant?
P1: That a society that differs in some way, that's split up in some way ... And some very important issue that would be terrible for Australia, and nearly start a revolution ...
P2: We're not used to having a lot of coloured people with us in this society. We've got them in the outskirts of country towns but not in the city, only a small minority.
T: [to P1] So you think quite clearly he was talking about black/white divisions, the 'split' was the word you used.
P1: Religions. I think, too, religious splitting, even national. Look at the Croatians, they seem to stick together from what we've heard.
T: Could be true of any division, if it was a large division ...

As in D 1, this lesson had frequent variations from the more common P/T/P/T/P/T order of turn-taking, with frequent P/P/P exchanges, that were not the result of pupil interjections. Both texts are also characterised by pupils interrupting teachers (other than by talking at the back of the room!). All this is evidence of the openness necessary for learners who are taking responsibility for 'making sense' of the subject matter. In this role, speakers may need to have some turn-taking flexibility to seek, opportunistically, to agree or disagree or request more information about the validity claims in the discourse.

Several new question types have made their appearance. There is the 'what do you think?' question (WDYT), to which pupils respond by giving their (often personal) views. There is the methodological challenge of 'Do you think that applies to everyone?', 'What is your evidence?' etc.; and the procedural 'Is that what you're saying?' and 'Do I understand you?'. Clearly a GSP for these sequences will display quite a lot of different moves from the previous groups from Boxes 1, 2 and 3. Some of these will be optional elements of their genres but some must be obligatory, such as when the question series proceeds by a series of WDYT questions.

Freire and Shor speak of 'inductive teaching', which is a similar idea to that being advanced here. In this kind of teaching, teachers, even critical teachers, have their goals. They are not aimless. In any case, teachers often work under constraints of syllabi and examinations. What is at stake is how these goals are reached and whether, in the reaching of the teacher's goals, there is room to reach some of the pupils' goals. Almost any subject can be refracted in various ways. There is always room for the pupils' own reality, if only as a starting point: 'My understanding is that dialogic inquiry is situated in the language, politics and themes of the students.'[15] This situating is a contextualising that recognises the simple reality — that pupils will start from what is real to them anyway. Freire calls this the difference between reading the word and reading the world: '... the world of reading is only the world of the schooling process, a closed world, cut off from the world where we have experiences'.[16]

But while the teacher must relate to this real world, she can also challenge it. This is the inductive moment, where, in terms of the argument of the present work, the teacher begins to draw the pupils into the discourse of the species, beyond their local culture. It is a delicate matter to do this and avoid becoming the '... manipulating, *domesticating* educator [who] always keeps in his or her *own* hands' the process and the conclusions (Freire). Ira Shor puts it this way: 'Distributing ownership ... to the students will be delicate, like transferring a property right, a political power and an intellectual facility all at once.'[17]

The teacher in GWTT 1 was unable to cope when she lost ownership of the direction of the lesson. At about half-way through the lesson, this teacher attempted to move to a mini-discussion with teacher as neutral chairperson:

T: Alright. You seem to know what a discussion is and the rules. Now I want you to try and put those rules into practice ... I'd like to know your thoughts on television ... Now, would anyone like to start the discussion?

P: Um, the ads.

T: What about the ads?

P: There's too many [etc.]

T: Alright. [Turning to another student with hand raised] What do you want to say on that?

P: They are only allowed to have ten an hour [etc. etc.]

T: OK.

P: Some shows interfere with other shows.

T: Ah, so specials interrupt normal viewing. You don't like that?

P: It's really bad [etc.]

T: Well all right. Let's ... what we should do is try and talk about not a whole lot of jagged ideas, but we'll talk about one thing at a time. Right. So Jill mentioned ads. Do any other people have ideas about ads before we go any further?

Now arguably, the teacher herself jumped about topically from home to playground to work and so on just as much as the pupils, but a switch of topic after three pupil comments on advertisements is perceived as 'jagged' by the teacher. An assembly of teacher questions with pupil answers left out can seem just as topically jagged. Try it. What is at stake is the ownership of the direction of the lesson, i.e. the problem. But again, arguably, the purpose of the lesson would be served just as well by a different strategy and one which recognised pupil problems and relevances.

The analysis can be carried out in much greater lexico-grammatical and structural detail and at a higher level of delicacy, but I think the point is made. There are a wide range of teacher agent roles and a wide range of ways of teaching. Any broad pedagogical function, such as 'revision', might be handled in quite different ways as far as pupil and teacher attitudes to their role as inquirers is concerned. We can ask critical questions about the form of teaching and learning, backed up by concrete and detailed linguistic analysis, and when we are accused of utopianism we can point to viable alternatives. To those who reply that certain subject matter must be covered, revised and tested, we can reply: 'It can be covered, revised and tested, but in a more or less critical way.'

Some might object that they cannot talk that way in *their* classrooms, to which it is possible to reply that *not* talking 'that way' is at least half of what makes their classrooms the way they are. We can return to the considerations with which we began. What sort of world do we want? What sort of problem-solving approaches do we want the next generation to have? We *can* explore these questions in a *practical* way through critical linguistics.

9 The Context of the Practical

We hear much talk nowadays about making education practical. We hear the same thing about teacher training. But when we dig a little deeper we uncover a rather strange notion of what 'being practical' means. It seems to mean avoiding theory rather than finding theory which really describes and explains different courses of human conduct. It seems to mean education which leads towards whatever it is the speaker wants to see happen. For 'practical' read 'leading to ever-increasing gross national product'. That is what is implicit in someone saying that something is 'economically desirable'. This phrase doesn't necessarily mean that the policy concerned is more economical or efficient. It merely means that it contributes to continued growth of *tradeable* goods and services — note: not all goods and services. For 'practical' read 'costing the government less per pupil' but without all that much attention to the quality as opposed to the quantity of educational output. For 'practical' read 'producing measurable outcomes in basic skills', without any recognition that some basic skills, like communicative competence, cannot be easily measured, and those that can be aren't necessarily more than a beginning of what we need to produce.

One of the reasons for the turn towards the practical, apart from those associated with the neo-conservative critique of intellectuals, is the perceived failure of educational research to throw light on the problems of classroom teachers. In fact, mainstream educational research *has* failed to deliver the goods. It is asking a great deal for me now to suggest to teachers that they turn to a new model of research and systematic reflection on practice, especially when mainstream research has for so long dismissed teachers' experience and craft knowledge. Which is not to say that all teachers' knowledge is a good basis for teaching and learning. The alternative to the 'dim view' of teachers' knowledge is not an acceptance of the mainstream of teaching and learning in our society. That is too deeply constrained by the difficult conditions with which teachers have to cope to provide a good model of better practice. Better practice, practice which is better than common practice, is rare, almost by definition, but at any given level of development, it is to the higher but still infrequent levels of practice that we must look.

The mainstream's impotence is a product of its own version of the method mistake. It is that mistake that led to a strategy for concept formation which dismissed participants' concepts in favour of technical ideas such as 'need for achievement', 'motivation', 'locus of control' and the like. This strategy contributed towards a teacher alienation from the language (jargon) of educational research.

The turn to qualitative research (recently being aped by the mainstream in its search for legitimacy) is reversing this trend. The qualitative research movement employs a phenomenological concept formation strategy; its concepts are either taken directly from teachers' concepts or are second order constructions from them. One of the corollaries of this shift in conceptual strategy is the recommendation on scientific grounds that teachers be involved in research in roles other than mere 'subjects' of research (for 'subjects' here read 'objects'). The role in research of the teacher as reflective practitioner — as in critical action research and related models — is one which makes teachers a part of the validation process rather than simply suppliers of data. To an extent, this underpins the practicality of the new research.

However, reflection is not something that occurs easily under conditions of constraint and pressure. Time out, the counsel of others, resources and opportunity to express new insights and have others react to them are all necessary parts of effective reflection. This can only occur in a supportive environment, where solitude, leisure and counsel are readily available. In-service 'retreats' can provide one such environment. Pre-service teacher education can provide another. In the first volume of this series, Corson provides a sensitive discussion of democratic reflection on school language policy.

But mainstream research might still have problems even were its conceptual strategy a more useful one; or, rather, now that the mainstream is adopting more useful research strategies, a problem remains which it shares with some versions of qualitative research. Research is always about questions, it is never just the way things are. Qualitative myopia is as bad as quantitative myopia. It is not only process/product research that focuses on how to teach whatever-it-is-that-someone-has-decided-should-be-taught or recommends 'solutions' to teaching problems that undermine motivation at another level. For instance, some of the methods recommended as a result of empiricist qualitative research into science teaching might help pupils acquire the concepts of physicists and to abandon their own, naive ideas, but at the same time make physics seem unreal and theoretical.

A naturalistic study of education cannot be simply and completely empiricist. It is inevitably a study of semiosis — making meaningful action. Naturalistic inquiry lays claim to identify the processes actually at work in a situation. It makes *ontological* claims. We should be wary of the blind faith of reductionist accounts of brains to cells to atoms to energy that influences some research programmes so far in advance of historically delivering actual explanations of human actions. We have perfectly good hermeneutic methods that every day yield workable insights into meanings and systems of meaning in language learning, reading and writing, and communication.

Pupil participation in learning is both observable and explicable, but variables such as 'time on task' are very crude indicators of it. It is explicable through functional linguistics because this is a linguistics that examines participation in task achievement through the examination of agent roles and the expected contribution of particular agents to task completion in the form of communicative moves. The communicative demands of particular teaching actions can be examined in terms of the agent role requirements, and the biographies of individuals or the cultures of their origin can be examined from the point of view of whether or not they provide the resources required. In conjunction with constitutive ethnography, systemics can provide a more sensitive and delicate model of learning participation and non-participation than the favourite child of neo-conservative educators — time on task. More importantly, a systemic analysis does something more than merely recommend that teachers somehow increase time on task. It permits identification of the obstacles to participation and guides experiments aimed at removing them. It also focuses on the *quality* of time spent, whereas time on task is a qualitatively crude variable; and finally, critical systemics recognises links between learning and motivation which other approaches are unable to identify.

This book began with a statement of our need for a truly universal problem-solving education. The problems we face will not yield to yesterday's methods. We must have global solutions and this necessity confronts us with an ultimate moral choice. The needed solutions can resemble the 'final solution' of Auschwitz or they can be based on some life-affirming notion of universal justice. Either we abandon the goal of more and more and still more economic growth for the already developed nations, *or* we pursue a policy of not only deliberately repressing the economic (and population) growth of poorer nations but also of exploiting the very resources they need for simple survival. If the 'greenhouse' predictions are right in only the general sense of the direction of global climatic change, and no new source of clean energy is found, *and* we continue our present politics, the price of clean air and a reasonable climate for us may be eventually genocidal for the rest of the world.

If we choose the alternative of a universally just solution, we choose to make great cultural changes in our own societies. If the inhabitants of China and India were to use as much electricity as we do, the rate of greenhouse and ozone-destroying emissions would increase more than 500%. How much must we change our lifestyle for them to increase their electricity consumption to half our level without increasing the rate of emissions? Questions like this focus our attention on the magnitude of the effects we must estimate and come to terms with. We must learn to value the things of the mind and the spirit more than television sets and fast cars.

But the approach to teaching and learning recommended in this book is not utopian unless you wish to say that the very existence of ideals is utopian. The recommendation that participants fashion critique and choose feasible reforms from within situations means that the group of people most likely to be utopian, intellectuals who do not have to live with their recommendations on a day to day basis, are not the ones who carry out actual critiques and create concrete changes in practices.

One of the delights we must also learn to love is intercultural communication and learning. The cultures of the microwave West desperately need to regain the delight in simple things, and in the spirit, which other cultures, less distant from the time when the world was enchanted with ultimate significance and meaning, still possess. In addition, it is only intercultural solutions which will be just solutions to our global problems. (I include here, and not whimsically, the intercultural divide between men and women and the global problem of just gender practices.)

The approach to the study of classroom talk adopted in this book is as well adapted to the study of intercultural communication as it is to monocultural situations. The contrast between the child's everyday knowledge and the knowledge of, say, professional scientists, is similar to that between culturally different interlocutors. We must choose whether we take as our model the typical authoritarian asymmetry of the scientist's communication with the layperson, or a discursive model. The former approach has already been with us for a long time, in the communicative relationship of imperial power with colonised cultures, and the imperialism of science and administrative rationality against everyday culture. Perhaps it is time we tried the alternative?

Notes

Chapter 1

1. Hanna Arendt, *The Human Condition*, Chicago: University of Chicago Press, 1958.
2. For a history of the Frankfurt School see M. Jay, *The Dialectical Imagination*, Boston: Little, Brown, 1973; and also see D. Held, *Introduction to Critical Theory: Horkheimer to Habermas*, London: Hutchison, 1980; R. Roderick, *Habermas and the Foundations of Critical Theory*, London: Macmillan, 1986; and Thomas McCarthy, *The Critical Theory of Jürgen Habermas*, London: Hutchison, 1978. For an account of the critical theory of education see R. Young, *A Critical Theory of Education: Habermas and Our Childrens' Future*, London: Harvester/Wheatsheaf Books, 1989 and New York: Teachers' College Press, 1990.
3. See the critique by G. Kortian, *Metacritique: The Philosophical Argument of Jürgen Habermas*, Cambridge: Cambridge University Press, 1980.
4. J. Dewey, *Democracy and Education*, New York: The Free Press, 1916, 1944.
5. Some recent examples: R. Bates, 'Is there a new paradigm in educational administration?', paper presented to the Annual Conference of the American Educational Research Association, 1988; J. H. Giroux, *Critical Theory and Educational Practice*, Geelong: Deakin University Press, 1983; W. Carr and S. Kemmis, *Becoming Critical: Knowing Through Action Research*, Geelong: Deakin University Press, 1983; S. Kemmis and L. Fitzclarence, *Curriculum Theorising: Beyond Reproduction Theory*, Geelong: Deakin University Press, 1986; S. Grundy, *Curriculum: Product or Praxis?* London: Falmer Press, 1986; and J. Smyth, *A Rationale for Teacher's Critical Pedagogy*, Geelong: Deakin University Press, 1987.
6. As set out in J. Habermas, *Knowledge and Human Interests*, London: Heinemann, 1968, and J. Habermas, *Zur Logik der Sozialwissensschaften*, Beiheft [Monograph] 5, *Philosophische Rundschau*, 14 (1966–7).
7. J. Habermas, *The Theory of Communicative Action*, Vol. 1, London: Heinemann, 1984, 375; hereafter called TCA.
8. Socrates in Plato's *Meno*.
9. I. Kant, *On Education*, Ann Arbor: University of Michigan Press, 1964, pp. 7–8.
10. See J. Habermas, *The Philosophical Discourse of Modernity* (PDM), Oxford: Polity Press, 1987 (original German version 1985); and R. Bernstein (ed.), *Habermas and Modernity*, Oxford: Polity Press, 1985. Also recent discussions in S. White, *The Recent Work of Jurgen Habermas: Reason, Justice and Modernity*, London: Cambridge University Press, 1986; and D. Ingram, *Habermas and the Dialectic of Reason*, London: Yale University Press, 1987.
11. PDM.
12. e.g. M. Van Maanen, 'Linking ways of knowing with ways of being practical', *Curriculum Inquiry* 6, 3 (1977), 205–28; J. Mezirow, 'A critical theory of adult education', *Adult Education* 32, 1 (1981), 3–24.

13. Immanent critique is discussed in D. Held, *Introduction to Critical Theory*.
14. See my discussion of indoctrination in 'Teaching equals indoctrination: The dominant epistemic practices of our schools', *British Journal of Educational Studies* 32, 3 (1984), 220–38.

Chapter 2

1. R. Descartes, *A Discourse on Method*, trans. J. Veitch, London: Dent, 1962, pp. 4 and 24.
2. H. Gadamer, *Truth and Method*, New York: The Seabury Press, 1975.
3. R. E. Young, 'A study of teacher epistemologies', *Australian Journal of Education* 25, 2 (1981), 194–208; 'The epistemic discourse of teachers: An ethnographic study', *Anthropology and Education Quarterly*, 12, 2 (1981).
4. J. Royce, *The Encapsulated Man*, Princeton: Van Nostrand, 1964.
5. I. Lakatos, 'Falsification and the methodology of scientific research programs', pp. 91–196 in I. Lakatos and A. Musgrave (eds), *Criticism and the Growth of Knowledge*, Cambridge: Cambridge University Press, 1970.
6. For a discussion of erotetics see J. Garrison and C. Macmillan, 'Erotetics and accountability', *Educational Theory* 37, 2 (1987), 295–301.
7. L. West and A. Pines (eds), *Cognitive Structures and Conceptual Change*, New York: Academic Press, 1985, p. 3.
8. Ibid., p. 6.
9. D. Perkins and G. Salomon, 'Are cognitive skills context-bound?' *Educational Researcher* 18, 1 (1989), 16–25.
10. J. Brown, A. Collins and P. Duguid, 'Situated cognition and the culture of learning', *Educational Researcher* 18, 1 (1989), 32–42, p. 33.
11. M. Miller, 'Learning how to contradict and still pursue a common end — the ontogenesis of moral argumentation', in J. Cook-Gumperz *et al.* (eds), *Children's Worlds and Children's Language*, Berlin: Mouton de Gruyter, 1986; and *Kollektive Lernprozesse*, Frankfurt: Suhrkamp, 1986.
12. C. Pontecorvo and C. Zuccermaglio, 'A passage to literacy: Learning in a social context', Ch. 4 in Y. Goodman (ed.), *Literacy Development*, New York: IRA, 1989, p. 1.
13. C. Pontecorvo, 'Interactions Socio-cognitives et Aquisition des Connaissances dans Interaction Scolaire', Congres Internationale de Fonctionement de l'enfant à l'école, Poitiers, 1987.
14. T. Adorno, 'Erziehung nach Auschwitz', in *Erziehung zur Mündigkeit*, Frankfurt: Suhrkamp, 1971.
Also cited in Chapter 2:
W. Quine, *Word and Object*, Cambridge, Mass.: Harvard University Press, 1964.

Chapter 3

1. J. Scudder and P. Mickunas, *Meaning, Dialogue and Enculturation*, Washington, DC: University Press of America, 1985.

Parts of this chapter are taken from my 'Habermas' ontology of learning: Reconstructing Dewey', *Educational Theory* 40, 4 (1990), with the permission of the Editor in Chief and the Trustees of the University of Illinois.

2. This lecture appeared as the postscript to the English edition of *Knowledge and Human Interests*.

3. e.g. A. Ferrara, 'A Critique of Habermas' Diskursethik', *Telos* 64, (1985), 45–74.

4. c.g. M. Van Maanen, 'Linking ways of knowing with ways of being practical'; J. Mezirow, 'A critical theory of adult education'.

5. J. Habermas, *The Theory of Communicative Action* (TCA), Vol. 1, p. 375.

6. Ibid., p. 378.

7. Ibid., pp. 75–102.

8. Ibid., pp. 220–2.

9. See T. Schatzki, 'The rationalization of meaning and understanding: Davidson and Habermas', *Synthese* 69 (1986), 51–79, for an account of Habermas' theory of meaning. Unfortunately, Schatzki mixes up Habermas' early and late work, so the account is not altogether adequate.

10. TCA, p. 106.

11. Ibid., pp. 106–7.

12. e.g. P. Murphy, 'Meaning, truth and ethical value', *Praxis International* 5, 3 (1985), 225–46, and 7, 1 (1987), 35–56.

13. As Schatzki points out, Habermas has this in common with Davidson.

14. As Jim Mackenzie suggested to me, the essentials of dialogue are the requirement to restore immediate consistency if violated and the requirement to defend a statement or give it up if challenged. But such a system is not based on mere description. To say that an argument is or is not valid etc. is not describing but participating in a dialogue. Cf: J. Hamblin, *Fallacies*, London: Macmillan, 1970, pp. 242–4.

15. Linguistic events — utterances — may be considered as tokens of linguistic types in the same way as less transient events, such as printed letters, may be. The utterance of noises that stand as a token for a sentence type would be an example of this. However, even if hearers of an utterance correctly identify the intended linguistic type, and understand its linguistic meaning, they will still have not fully attained to the utterer's meaning in making the utterance when and under whatever circumstances it was uttered. The notion of utterance meaning used here is similar to Grice's 'occasion meaning': 'Utterer's meaning, sentence-meaning and word-meaning', *Foundations of Language* 4, 1 (1968), 215–25. See also J. Perry, 'Cognitive significance and new theories of reference', *Nous* 22, 1 (1988), 1–19.

16. TCA, Vol. 1, pp. 80–120.

17. Ibid., pp. 85–6, 101.

18. Ibid., p. 101.

19. Adapted from TCA, Vol. 1, p. 329.

20. Ibid., p. 87, *et passim*.

21. Ibid., p. 99.

22. Ibid., pp. 100–1.

23. J. Dewey, 'Knowledge and speech reaction', in *Dewey and His Critics*, ed. S. Morgenbesser, New York: *The Journal of Philosophy*, 1977 (originally published in 1922), p. 458.

24. In Dewey's special sense.

25. As was also observed by F. Olafson, 'The school and society: Dewey's philosophy of education', in S, Cahn (ed.), *New Studies in the Philosphy of John Dewey*, Hanover, NH: University Press of New England, 1977, pp. 172–204.
26. In the first part of TCA, Vol. 2.
27. *Experience and Nature*, New York: W. W. Norton, 1929, p. 299.
28. Habermas, *Communication and the Evolution of Society*, London: Heinemann, 1979, p. 160.
29. Not that Dewey didn't have this in mind. The issue is whether his analysis of communication was complete and whether his emphasis on it was consistent.

Also cited in Chapter 3:

J. Dewey, *Democracy and Education*.

J. Thompson and D. Held (eds), *Habermas: Critical Debates*, London: Macmillan, 1982.

Chapter 4

1. J. Habermas, *Communication and the Evolution of Society* (CES), Ch. 1.
   Also see R. Young, 'Critical teaching and learning', *Educational Theory* 38, 1 (1988), 47–59, and 'Moral development, ego autonomy and questions of practicality in the critical theory of schooling', *Educational Theory* 38, 4 (1988), 391–404, for further discussion of the ISS. Parts of the latter have been incorporated in revised form in the latter part of this chapter, with the permission of the Editor in Chief and the Trustees of the University of Illinois.
2. J. Habermas, 'On systematically distorted communication', *Inquiry* 13 (1970), 205–18.
3. See Habermas, ibid. and R. Young, *A Critical Theory of Education*, pp. 75–9.
4. This is a concept of ideology which does not simply equate it with someone's set of ideas, as relativists do (everyone has an ideology), nor one which assumes a valid standpoint made up of correct theory, as, say, some Marxists do, but a procedural one, based on the structural make-up of the group constructing ideology and the interests involved.
5. R. Spaemann, 'Emanzipation — ein Bildungziel?' *Merkur* 29, 320 (1975), 11–24.
6. J. Oelkers, 'Paedagogische Anmerkungen zu Habermas' Theorie des kommunikativen Handelns', *Zeitschrift für Padagogik* 30, 2 (1983), 271–80.
7. R. Graham Oliver, 'Through the doors of reason: Dissolving four paradoxes of education', *Educational Theory* 35, 1 (1985), 17.
8. As described by R. Young in 'Critical theory and classroom questioning', *Language and Education* 1, 2 (1987), 125–34.
9. J. S. Mill, *On Liberty*, London: Dent, 1910, p. 73.
10. R. Peters, 'Reason and habit: The paradox of moral education', W. Niblett in (ed.), *Moral Education in a Changing Society*, London: Faber and Faber, 1963, p. 271.
11. R. S. Peters, 'Freedom and the development of the free man', in J. Doyle (ed.), *Educational Judgments*, London: Routledge and Kegan Paul, 1973, p. 135.
12. Peters, 'Reason and habit', p. 271.
13. J. Dewey, *The Child and the Curriculum*, Chicago: University of Chicago Press, 1900, 1956, p. 15.
14. See Habermas' *Communication and the Evolution of Society*, p. 85. His use of Kohlberg raises many questions. Habermas himself is well aware of the many

difficulties of genetic structuralism, and of the circularity that afflicts the theory–data relationship in this kind of research (e.g. *Moralbewusstsein und kommunikatives Handeln*, Frankfurt: Suhrkamp, 1983, pp. 49–50 and 183–200). He notes a number of problems of Kohlbergian theory and discusses the relationship between developmental psychology and his rational reconstruction of universal developmental possibilities. It may be sufficient for the purposes of this discussion to express a caveat concerning the adequacy of expressing development in stage terms.

15. M. Miller, 'Learning how to contradict and still pursue a common end' and *Kollektive Lernprozesse*.
16. *Kollektive Lernprozesse*, p. 447.
17. J. Dewey, *The Child and the Curriculum*, p. 15.
18. e.g. M. Halliday and R. Hasan, *Language, Context and Text*, Geelong: Deakin University Press, 1985.
19. J. Brown, A. Collins and P. Duguid, 'Situated cognition and the culture of learning'.
20. J. Dewey, *Democracy and Education*, p. 9.

Chapter 5

1. Habermas, TCA, Vol. 1, p. 138.
2. Ibid.
3. Ibid., p. 330.
4. Ibid., p. 297.
5. T. Ballmer and W. Brennenschul, *Speech Act Classification*, Heidelberg: Springer, 1981.
6. D. Wunderlich, *Grunglagen der Linguistik*, Hamburg, 1974.
7. See also the critique of language act theory by J. Edmondson, *Spoken Discourse: A Model for Analysis*, London: Longmans, 1981.
8. Sbisa and Fabbri, and A. Cicourel, cited in R. Hasan, 'What's going on: A dynamic view of context in language', paper delivered to the LACAS Forum, 1980, p. 6.
9. R. Hasan, 'What's going on', p. 6.
10. J. Martin, 'Lexical cohesion, field and genre', in T. Threadgold *et al.* (eds), *Semiotics, Ideology, Language*, Sydney: Sydney Studies in Society and Culture, No. 3, 1986.
11. For a discussion see D. Corson, *Education for Work*, Palmerston North: The Dunmore Press, 1988, Ch. 4.
12. G. Kress, *Linguistic Processes in Socio-cultural Practice*, Geelong: Deakin University Press, 1985.
13. Ibid., p. 3.
14. Ibid., p. 6.
15. Ibid., p. 6.
16. Ibid., p. 4.
17. Ibid., p. 5.
18. R. Hasan, 'The ontogenesis of ideology: An interpretation of mother–child talk,' in T. Threadgold *et al.* (eds), *Semiotics, Ideology, Language*, p. 126.
19. Ibid., pp. 137–8.
20. Ibid.

Chapter 6

1. e.g. M. Gregory and S. Carroll, *Language and Situation*, London: Routledge and Kegan Paul, 1968; D. Hymes, 'The ethnography of speaking', in J. Fishman (ed.), *Readings in the Sociology of Language*, The Hague: Mouton, 1968; and see D. Corson, *Language Policy Across the Curriculum*, Clevedon: Multilingual Matters, 1990, pp. 118–19.
2. M. Halliday and R. Hasan, *Language, Context and Text*.
3. Ibid., p. 60.
4. Ibid., p. 57.
5. Ibid., p. 63.
6. Ibid., p. 61.
7. L. Smith and W. Geoffrey, *The Complexities of an Urban Classroom*, New York: Holt, Rinehart and Winston, 1968.
8. D. Barnes *et al.*, *Language, the Learner and the School*, Harmondsworth: Penguin, 1969.
9. K. Gambley, 'Contexts for sharing news', B.Ed. Honours Long Essay, Faculty of Education, The University of Sydney, 1989.
10. J. Dewey, *Democracy and Education*, p. 5.
11. R. Roth, 'Practical use of language in the school', *Language Arts* 63, 2 (1986), 134–42.
12. Ibid., p. 140.
13. Ibid., p. 141.
14. J. Dewey, *Democracy and Education*, p. 217.

Chapter 7

1. R. Stevens, *The Question as a Measure of Efficiency in Instruction*, New York: Teachers' College, 1912, p. 16.
    For a discussion of research on classroom talk see R. E. Young *et al.*, 'Linguistic models of teaching and learning', *International Encyclopedia of Education*, London: Pergamon Press, 1985; and for a history of research to 1966 see J. Hoetker and W. Ahlbrand, 'The persistence of the recitation', *American Educational Research Journal* 6, 2 (1969), 145–67.
2. A. McHoul, 'The organization of turns at formal talk in the classroom', *Language in Society* 7 (1978), 183–213.
3. See J. Green, 'Exploring classroom discourse', *Educational Psychology* 18, 3 (1983), 180–99.
4. P. Woods (ed.), *Pupil Strategies: Explorations in the Sociology of the School*, London: Croom Helm, 1980.
5. F. Erickson and J. Schultz, 'When is a context: Some issues and methods in the analysis of social competence', pp. 147–60 in J. Green and C. Wallat (eds), *Ethnography and Language in Educational Settings*, New Jersey: Ablex, 1981, pp. 151, 152.
6. J. Sinclair and M. Coulthard, *Towards an Analysis of Discourse: The English used by Teachers and Pupils*, Oxford: Oxford University Press, 1975.
7. Ibid., p. 108.
8. J. Edmondson, *Spoken Discourse: A Model for Analysis*.

9.   H. Mehan, 'Structuring school structure', *Harvard Education Review* 48 (1978), 32–64; also P. Griffin and F. Humphrey, *Talk and Task at Lesson Time*, New York: Carnegie Corporation, 1980.

Chapter 8

1.   See an excellent discussion of many issues in P. Freire and I. Shor, *A Pedagogy for Liberation*, London: Macmillan, 1987, especially pp. 146–8, p. 147. See also R. E. Young, 'Critical theory and classroom questioning'.
2.   K. Watson and R. Young, 'Discourse for learning in the classroom', *Language Arts* 63, 2 (1986), 126–33, p. 129.
3.   P. Griffin and F. Humphrey, *Talk and Task at Lesson Time*; and J. Sinclair and M. Coulthard, *Towards an Analysis of Discourse*, pp. 51, 53–4.
4.   A. Edwards and V. Furlong, *The Language of Teaching*, London: Heinemann, 1978, p. 108; also Edwards and N. Mercer, *Common Knowledge: The Development of Understanding in the Classroom*, London: Methuen, 1987 (for a useful parallel account to mine).
5.   Ibid., pp. 41–2.
6.   J. Edmondson, *Spoken Discourse: A Model for Analysis*, pp. 34–8.
7.   See Griffin and Humphrey, *Talk and Task*.
8.   K. Watson and R. Young, 'Teacher reformations of pupil discourse', *Australian Review of Applied Linguistics* 3, 2 (1980), 37–47.
9.   P. Freire and I. Shor, *A Pedagogy for Liberation*, p. 104.
10. See K. Watson and R. Young, 'Teacher reformulations of pupil discourse', p. 44.
11. W. Chafe, 'Creativity in verbalisation: Its implications for the nature of stored knowledge', in R. Freedle (ed.), *Discourse Production and Comprehension*, New Jersey: Ablex, 1977, pp. 51–2.
12. G. Jefferson, 'On exposed and embedded correction in conversation', in G. Button and J. Lee (eds), *Talk and Social Organisation*, Clevedon: Multilingual Matters, 1987.
13. Watson and Young, 'Teacher reformations'.
14. See Griffin and Humphrey, *Talk and Task*.
15. Freire and Shor, *A Pedagogy for Liberation*, p. 104.
16. Ibid., p. 135.
17. Ibid., p. 160.

Bibliography

ADORNO, T. 1971, Erziehung nach Auschwitz. In *Erziehung zur Mündigkeit*. Frankfurt: Suhrkamp.

ARENDT, H. 1958, *The Human Condition*. Chicago: University of Chicago Press.

BALLMER, T. and BRENNENSCHUL, W. 1981, *Speech Act Classification*. Heidelberg: Springer.

BARNES, D. *et al.* 1969, *Language, the Learner and the School*. Harmondsworth: Penguin.

BATES, R. 1988, Is there a new paradigm in educational administration? Paper presented to the Annual Conference of the American Educational Research Association.

BERNSTEIN, R. (ed.) 1985 *Habermas and Modernity*. Oxford: Polity Press.

BROWN, J., COLLINS, A. and DUGUID, P. 1989, Situated cognition and the culture of learning. *Educational Researcher* 18, 1, 32–42.

BUTTON, G. and LEE, J. 1987, *Talk and Social Organisation*. Clevedon: Multilingual Matters.

CARR, W. and KEMMIS, S. 1983, *Becoming Critical: Knowing through Action Research*. Geelong: Deakin University Press.

CHAFE, W. 1977, Creativity in verbalisation: Its implications for the nature of stored knowledge. In R. FREEDLE (ed.), *Discourse Production and Comprehension*. New Jersey: Ablex.

COOK-GUMPERZ, J. *et al.*(eds) 1986, *Children's Worlds and Children's Language*. Berlin: Mouton de Gruyter.

CORSON, D. 1988, *Oral Language Across the Curriculum*. Clevedon: Multilingual Matters.

— 1988, *Education for Work*. Palmerston North: The Dunmore Press.

— 1990, *Language Policy Across the Curriculum*. Clevedon: Multilingual Matters.

DANNEQUIN, C. 1987, Les Enfants Baillonnes: The teaching of French as mother tongue in elementary school. *Language and Education* 1, 1, 15–31.

DESCARTES, R. 1962, *A Discourse on Method*, Trans. J. Veitch. London: Dent.

DEWEY, J. 1900, 1956, *The Child and the Curriculum*. Chicago: University of Chicago Press.

— 1916, 1944, *Democracy and Education*. New York: The Free Press.

— 1922, 1977, Knowledge and speech reaction. In S. MORGENBESSER (ed.), *Dewey and His Critics*. New York: *The Journal of Philosophy*.

— 1929, *Experience and Nature*. New York: W. W. Norton.

EDMONDSON, J. 1981, *Spoken Discourse: A Model for Analysis*. London: Longmans.

EDWARDS, A. and FURLONG, V. 1978, *The Language of Teaching*. London: Heinemann.

EDWARDS, A. and MERCER, N. 1987, *Common Knowledge: The Development of Understanding in the Classroom*. London: Methuen.

ERICKSON, F. and SCHULTZ, J. 1981, When is a context: Some issues and methods in the analysis of social competence. In J. GREEN and C. WALLAT (eds), *Ethnography and Language in Educational Settings*. New Jersey: Ablex, pp. 147–60.

FERRARA, A. 1985, A critique of Habermas' Diskursethik. *Telos* 64, 45–74.

FREIRE, P. and SHOR, I. 1987, *A Pedagogy for Liberation*. London: Macmillan.

GADAMER, H. 1975, *Truth and Method*. New York: The Seabury Press.

GAMBLEY, K. 1989, 'Contexts for sharing news'. B.Ed. Honours Long Essay, Faculty of Education, The University of Sydney.

GARRISON, J. and MACMILLAN, C. 1987, Erotetics and accountability. *Educational Theory* 37, 2, 295–301.

GIROUX, J. H. 1983, *Critical Theory and Educational Practice*. Geelong: Deakin University.

GREEN, J. 1983, Exploring classroom discourse. *Educational Psychology* 18, 3, 180–99.

GREGORY, M. and CARROLL, S. 1968, *Language and Situation*. London: Routledge and Kegan Paul.

GRICE, J. 1968, Utterer's meaning, sentence-meaning and word-meaning. *Foundations of Language* 4, 1, 215–25.

GRIFFIN, P. and HUMPHREY, F. 1980, *Talk and Task at Lesson Time*. New York: Carnegie Corporation.

GRUNDY, S. 1986, *Curriculum: Product or Praxis?* London: Falmer Press.

HABERMAS, J. 1966–7, *Zur Logik der Sozialwissensschaften*. Beiheft [Monograph] 5, *Philosophische Rundschau* 14.

— 1968, *Knowledge and Human Interests*. London: Heinemann.

— 1970, On systematically distorted communication. *Inquiry* 13, 205–18.

— 1979, *Communication and the Evolution of Society*. London: Heinemann.

— 1983, *Moralbewusstsein und kommunikatives Handeln*. Frankfurt: Suhrkamp.

— 1984, *The Theory of Communicative Action*, Vol. 1. London: Heinemann.

— 1987, *The Philosophical Discourse of Modernity*. Oxford: Polity Press (original German version 1985).

HALLIDAY, M. and HASAN, R. 1985 *Language, Context and Text*. Geelong: Deakin University Press.

HAMBLIN, J. 1970, *Fallacies*. London: Macmillan.

HASAN, R. 1980, What's going on: A dynamic view of context in language. Paper delivered to the LACAS Forum.

— 1986, The ontogenesis of ideology: An interpretation of mother–child talk. In T. THREADGOLD *et al.* (eds), *Semiotics, Ideology, Language*. Sydney: Sydney Studies in Society and Culture Series, No. 3.

HELD, D. 1980, *An Introduction to Critical Theory: Horkheimer to Habermas*. London: Hutchison.

HOETKER, J. and AHLBRAND, W. 1969, The persistence of the recitation. *American Educational Research Journal* 6, 2, 145–67.

HYMES, D. 1968, The ethnography of speaking. In J. FISHMAN (ed.), *Readings in the Sociology of Language*. The Hague: Mouton.

INGRAM, D. 1987, *Habermas and the Dialectic of Reason*. London: Yale University Press.

JAY, M. 1973, *The Dialectical Imagination*. Boston: Little, Brown.

JEFFERSON, G. 1987, On exposed and embedded correction in conversation. In G. BUTTON and J. LEE (eds), *Talk and Social Organisation*. Clevedon: Multilingual Matters.

KANT, I. 1964, *On Education*. Ann Arbor: University of Michigan Press.

KEMMIS, S. and FITZCLARENCE, L. 1986, *Curriculum Theorising: Beyond Reproduction Theory*. Geelong: Deakin University Press.

KORTIAN, G. 1980, *Metacritique: The Philosophical Argument of Jürgen Habermas*. Cambridge: Cambridge University Press.

KRESS, G. 1985, *Linguistic Processes in Socio-cultural Practice*. Geelong: Deakin University Press.

LAKATOS, I. 1970, Falsification and the methodology of scientific research programs. In I. LAKATOS and A. MUSGRAVE (eds), *Criticism and the Growth of Knowledge*. Cambridge: Cambridge University Press, pp. 91–196.

MARGOLIS, J. 1977, The relevance of Dewey's epistemology. In S. CAHN (ed.), *New Studies in the Philosophy of John Dewey*. Hanover, New Hampshire: University Press of New England, pp. 117–48, 121.

MARTIN, J. 1986, Lexical cohesion, field and genre. In T. THREADGOLD *et al.* (eds), *Semiotics, Ideology, Language*. Sydney: Sydney Studies in Society and Culture, No. 3.

MCCARTHY, T. 1978, *The Critical Theory of Jürgen Habermas*. London: Hutchison.

MCHOUL, A. 1978, The organization of turns at formal talk in the classroom. *Language in Society* 7, 183–213.

MEHAN, H. 1978, Structuring school structure. *Harvard Education Review* 48, 32–64.

MEZIROW, J. 1981, A critical theory of adult education. *Adult Education* 32, 1, 3–24.

MILL, J. 1910, *On Liberty*. London: Dent.

MILLER, M. 1986, Learning how to contradict and still pursue a common end — the ontogenesis of moral argumentation. In J. COOK-GUMPERZ *et al.*(eds), *Children's Worlds and Children's Language*. Berlin: Mouton de Gruyter.

— 1986, *Kollektive Lernprozesse*. Frankfurt: Suhrkamp.

MURPHY, P. 1985, 1987, Meaning, truth and ethical value. *Praxis International* 5, 3, 225–46; and 7, 1, 35–56.

OELKERS, J. 1983, Paedagogische Anmerkungen zu Habermas' Theorie des kommunikativen Handelns. *Zeitschrift für Padagogik* 30, 2, 271–80.

OLAFSON, F. 1977, The school and society: Dewey's philosophy of education. In S. CAHN (ed.), *New Studies in the Philosophy of John Dewey*. Hanover, NH: University Press of New England, pp. 172–204.

OLIVER, R. GRAHAM 1985, Through the doors of reason: Dissolving four paradoxes of education. *Educational Theory* 35, 1, 17.

PERKINS, D. and SALOMON, G. 1989, Are cognitive skills context-bound? *Educational Researcher* 18, 1, 16–25.

PERRY, J. 1988, Cognitive significance and new theories of reference. *Nous* 22, 1, 1–19.

PETERS, R. 1963, Reason and habit: The paradox of moral education. In W. NIBLETT (ed.), *Moral Education in a Changing Society*. London: Faber and Faber.

— 1973, Freedom and the development of the free man. In J. DOYLE (ed.), *Educational Judgments*. London: Routledge and Kegan Paul.

PONTECORVO, C. and ZUCCERMAGLIO, C. 1989, A passage to literacy: Learning in a social context. Chapter 4 in Y. GOODMAN (ed.), *Literacy Development*. New York: IRA.

PONTECORVO, C. 1987, Interactions Socio-cognitives et Aquisition des Connaissances in Interaction Scolaire. Congres Internationale de Fonctionement de l'enfant à l'école, Poitiers.

QUINE, W. 1964, *Word and Object*. Cambridge, Mass.: Harvard University Press.

RODERICK, R. 1986, *Habermas and the Foundations of Critical Theory*. London: Macmillan.

ROTH, R. 1986, Practical use of language in the school. *Language Arts* 63, 2, 134–42.

ROYCE, J. 1964, *The Encapsulated Man*. Princeton: Van Nostrand.

SBISA, FABBRI and CICOUREL, A., cited in R. HASAN 1980, What's going on: A dynamic view of context in language. Paper delivered to the LACAS Forum.

SCHATZKI, T. 1986, The rationalization of meaning and understanding: Davidson and Habermas. *Synthese* 69, 51–79.

SCUDDER, J. and MICKUNAS, P. 1985, *Meaning, Dialogue and Enculturation*. Washington, DC: University Press of America.

SINCLAIR, J. and COULTHARD, M. 1975, *Towards an Analysis of Discourse: The English used by Teachers and Pupils*. Oxford: Oxford University Press.

SMITH, L. and GEOFFREY, W. 1968, *The Complexities of an Urban Classroom*. New York: Holt, Rinehart and Winston.

SMYTH, J. 1987, *A Rationale for Teacher's Critical Pedagogy*. Geelong: Deakin University Press.

SPAEMANN, R. 1975, Emanzipation — ein Bildungziel? *Merkur* 29, 320, 11–24.

STEVENS, R. 1912, *The Question as a Measure of Efficiency in Instruction*. New York: Teachers' College.

THOMPSON, J. and HELD, D. (eds) 1982, *Habermas: Critical Debates*. London: Macmillan.

THREADGOLD, T. *et al.* (eds) 1986, *Semiotics, Ideology, Language*. Sydney: Sydney Studies in Society and Culture Series, No. 3.

VAN MAANEN, M. 1977, Linking ways of knowing with ways of being practical. *Curriculum Inquiry* 6, 3, 205–28.

WATSON, K. and YOUNG, R. 1980, Teacher reformulations of pupil discourse. *Australian Review of Applied Linguistics* 3, 2, 37–47.

— 1986, Discourse for learning in the classroom. *Language Arts* 63, 2, 126–33.

WEST, L. and PINES, A. (eds) 1985, *Cognitive Structures and Conceptual Change*. New York: Academic Press.

WHITE, S. 1986, *The Recent Work of Jurgen Habermas: Reason, Justice and Modernity*. London: Cambridge University Press.

WOODS, P. (ed.) 1980, *Pupil Strategies: Explorations in the Sociology of the School*. London: Croom Helm.

WUNDERLICH, D. 1974, *Grunglagen der Linguistik*. Hamburg:

YOUNG, R. 1981, A study of teacher epistemologies. *Australian Journal of Education* 25, 2, 194–208.

— 1981, The epistemic discourse of teachers: An ethnographic study. *Anthropology and Education Quarterly* 12, 2.

— 1984, Teaching equals indoctrination: The dominant epistemic practices of our schools. *British Journal of Educational Studies* 32, 3, 220–38.

— 1987, Critical·theory and classroom questioning. *Language and Education* 1, 2, 125–34.

— 1988, Critical teaching and learning. *Educational Theory* 38, 1, 47–59.

— 1988, Moral development, ego autonomy and questions of practicality in the critical theory of schooling. *Educational Theory* 38, 4, 391–404.

— 1989/90, *A Critical Theory of Education: Habermas and Our Children's Future*. London: Harvester/Wheatsheaf Books, 1989 and New York: Teachers' College Press, 1990.

— 1990, Habermas' ontology of learning: reconstructing Dewey. *Educational Theory* 40, 4, 471–82.

YOUNG, R. *et al.* 1985, Linguistic models of teaching and learning. *International Encyclopedia of Education*. London: Pergamon Press.

Index

Note: Page references in italics indicate tables.